The Omega Files

Tony Pearce

New Wine Press

New Wine Press
PO Box 17
Chichester
England PO20 6YB

ISBN: 1 903725 18 6

Typeset by CRB Associates, Reepham, Norfolk.
Printed in England by Clays Ltd, St Ives plc.

Contents

Introduction

Out of the Sixties

'This is brinkmanship. We could be on the brink of a third world war.'

The year was 1962. The place was a classroom in Bedford School. The event in question was the Cuban missile crisis when the United States and the Soviet Union confronted each other over the Soviet intention to put nuclear missiles on Cuba. I was 16 years old, studying for my 'A' levels and we were having a lesson called 'World Affairs'. Our teacher, Mr Eyre, walked in and began his lesson with this dramatic announcement.

As I sat there a flood of thoughts rushed through my brain. Could there really be a nuclear war? If so what chance had we got of survival? What kind of a crazy world is it in which the whole future of the human race can be decided by a handful of politicians over whom ordinary people like me have no control at all? What is the point of my studying to pass these exams and get on in the world if someone I don't know can press a button and blow us all up in a moment of time? Above all, what is to be done about it?

From that moment on a change came over my thinking. The possibility of doomsday entered my mind and I began to look for some way to make sense of the world, which had become so threatening to my future. Two thoughts began to take root – one to experience as much as I could of life and two to try to change the world. The results pushed me towards the counter-culture of the sixties. I hitch-hiked round Europe and beyond in the summer holidays, getting as far as Istanbul, Turkey one year and Tangier, Morocco, the next year. I listened to music by The Beatles and Bob Dylan and agreed that *All you need is love* and *The times they are a changin'*. The new road of a world without war and competition beckoned to me with its promises of peace, love and socialism.

By 1967 I was studying Modern Languages (French and German) at Cambridge University. French existentialist writers like Jean Paul Sartre and Albert Camus appealed to my way of thinking, although their philosophy led to the depressing conclusion that life had no real meaning. I had also spent some time in Germany. While I was there one of the big questions which came to me, as I stayed with a German family, was, 'How was it possible that these people who seemed so ordinary and not so different from us could have followed a madman like Hitler?' When I asked my hosts this question, the mother of the family said, 'You have no idea what it was like to stand in one of Hitler's rallies and feel the power that came out from his eyes.'

The question of Nazi Germany raised other questions I was grappling with: 'Why do people always pick on the Jews? What is it about these people that causes such hatred?' At school and at university I had Jewish friends and felt sympathy towards Jewish people. In May 1967 I was revising for my second year exams when the news came through of the build up of Arab forces on the borders of Israel. The newspapers were predicting a war against Israel and I read of Nasser of Egypt threatening to drive the Jews into the sea. I felt deeply involved in the issue and for some reason, which I could not quite explain, I wanted to help Israel.

One day I hitch-hiked down to London and went to an Israeli agency and offered to go out to help Israel if there was a war. My parents were understandably horrified at this idea and as it turned out, when war did break out in June, Israel did very well in six days without any help from me. As the

Israelis went into Jerusalem I knew that something very important had happened, although I did not know why.

By 1969 I had finished my studies and was now working as a teacher. I had changed my course in my final year at Cambridge and graduated with a degree in English. I ended up teaching English at a Grammar School in Retford, Nottinghamshire, a place I had never heard of before. To be honest I did not find Retford the most exciting place in the world and as I knew no one in the town I became quite lonely. But I had so much work to do preparing lessons and marking books that I really did not have time for much else except the job.

I had an 'A' level English class to teach and found some outlet for my interests in using my lessons to inject a bit of Marxist philosophy into these boys. There were two boys who were quite resistant to my ideas, however. They annoyed me greatly by coming into class wearing little badges, which said, 'Jesus lives'. It turned out they went to a local Pentecostal church, which I concluded must be some kind of a weird cult as I had never heard people from the Anglican church I had been to in my youth going on about Jesus in the way these boys did.

One day I set the class an essay to write on any book that had influenced them. I had not thought this one through, because what I got from these two boys was two long essays full of quotations from the Bible. Things like: *'All have sinned and come short of the glory of God'* and *'The wages of sin is death but the gift of God is eternal life'* and *'You must be born again'*.

'This is serious,' I thought. 'These guys are trying to convert me. Never mind, I know what to do. I have been to university and studied all kinds of thinkers and writers. I'll soon cure them of this infantile delusion of believing in God. We'll have a debate in the library and I'll show them why they should not believe.'

I really don't remember what I said at the debate, but I do remember that about half way through the proceedings I had a sinking feeling that I did not know what I was talking about. One of the boys, Alec, said how he had come to know

God personally through faith in Jesus Christ and how he communicated with God in prayer. Suddenly it came to me that they had been brainwashed into this by their parents and so I said, 'That's just your subjective experience. There is no objective evidence for the existence of God.'

They then said that the Bible is full of prophecies which cannot be explained without the supernatural foreknowledge of God and that there were even prophecies being fulfilled today relating to the second coming of Christ.

'Oh yeah? Like what?' I asked sceptically.

'It says in the Bible that the Jews will go back to Israel and that there will be a lot of trouble over Jerusalem and then Jesus will come back.'

Israel, Jerusalem, the Jews. My mind raced back two years to the 1967 Six-Day War and I wondered if that was the reason I had felt that there was something so important about that event. Without admitting it to the boys I knew that I had lost this debate and had to get myself better informed about why I should not believe the Bible. So why not buy a Bible and start reading it to be better able to say why it is a collection of fairy tales?

This event happened towards the end of the summer term. In the summer holidays it so happened that I had fixed up to go on a international youth conference organised by the Quakers in Sheffield at which there would be delegates from Britain, the USA and the Soviet Union. The idea was to do some work on a youth club in a deprived area and also to have political discussions about world peace. I did not have much time to read the Bible before I was pitched into high-powered discussions with the group about world events and how to create peace and a better world for the future.

We talked about the big political events of the time and I was really in my element telling both the Americans and the Soviets how they needed to sort out their countries and get their troops out of Vietnam and Czechoslovakia respectively. Before long I had established myself on the left politically which made me interesting to the Soviet delegation. They were all good Communists, because at that time it was impossible to get a visa to travel outside the Soviet Union without the approval of the Communist authorities.

A very attractive Russian girl called Lara was openly flirting with me and on one occasion when we were alone, she asked me, 'Do you believe in God, Tony?'

'I'm not sure,' I answered.

'In the Soviet Union all progressive young people do not believe in God,' she replied. 'To make a better world we have to do it without God and religion.'

I felt a battle going on inside me. During the three weeks of this conference I found myself increasingly moving away from God and the Bible and beginning to commit myself to Communism. I remember sitting in a park in Sheffield on my own and renouncing God in favour of the revolution.

Because I was not happy in Retford, I had already handed in my notice at the school there and got myself a job at a comprehensive school in west London. This school was much more multi-racial than the school in Retford with many Asian pupils. I hoped they would be more receptive to my left wing ideas and that they would realise that the answer to racial prejudice was a socialist society. I went to lectures on world revolution at London University and joined demonstrations about Vietnam and South Africa and was excited at the prospect of really getting involved in the radical left scene in London.

But however hard I tried to get away from God, I found that he kept popping up all over the place. One day I was going home from work on the underground and in front of me was a poster with a Bible verse on it. It said,

> *'But know this, that in the last days perilous times will come; for men will be lovers of themselves, lovers of money, boasters, proud, blasphemers, disobedient to parents, un-thankful, unholy, unloving, unforgiving, slanderers, without self-control, brutal, despisers of good, traitors, headstrong, haughty, lovers of pleasure, rather than lovers of God.'*
>
> (2 Timothy 3:1–4)

Again thoughts went racing through my mind. 'In the last days! And that's a pretty good description of people today. Suppose Jesus is coming back and I don't believe in him. What will happen to me? Suppose he comes back while I'm riding in this underground train. Don't be stupid. Of course Jesus isn't coming back. It's a fantasy. Forget it.'

But the thought would not go away. I went to a demonstration about the Vietnam War outside the US Embassy in Grosvenor Square, London. I was standing there with a placard saying, 'US Imperialists out of Vietnam!' when a girl went by giving out leaflets. Not an unusual occurrence as these demos were places where all kinds of groups were handing out information trying to get you to join their faction working for the great and glorious revolution. But this leaflet was a bit different. It began with a quote from the South American Marxist icon of the 1960s, Che Guevara:

> '*Hasta la Victoria Siempre*' – 'Until the Everlasting Victory'
>
> We must uproot all injustice, hatred, greed and bitterness . . .. in ourselves.
>
> The revolution must begin where the problems begin . . . in human hearts.
>
> Marx says change society and people will change as a result.
>
> Jesus says, '*You must be born again*', not physically but spiritually, for:
>
>> '*If anyone is in Christ Jesus he is a new creation,*
>> *the old has gone, the new has come.*'
>>
>> (2 Corinthians 5:17 NIV)
>
> Think about it. Decide for yourself who is right.
>
> '*Viva la Victoria Siempre.*'

I did not say anything to this girl but as I read this leaflet I knew deep down that it was true. The communist experiment had been a miserable failure, promising to free people from the chains of 'hatred, greed and fear' but in fact binding those chains ever more tightly around the people in dictatorships which crushed and oppressed the people and gave power to the clique who gained control of the Communist Party.

At the time I had just been reading a book, called *The New Class* by a Yugoslav writer called Milovan Djilas, who helped to bring the Communists to power in Yugoslavia after the war and for a time was second in command to Tito. Then he fell from favour and became a dissident protesting at the corruption of power in the Stalinist Communist regimes of Eastern Europe. The basic idea of his book was that in power the Communists transformed themselves from being a revolutionary movement working for the rights of the people into a selfish bureaucracy concentrating power and wealth in their own hands and passing on their privileges to their children. In fact they became the new ruling class. He pointed out that there is something flawed in human character, which means that we cannot attain our ideals, and end up corrupting ourselves and everything we touch because of human selfishness.

As I read this leaflet and thought about the book by Djilas, it began to dawn on me that the problem of humanity really is what is inside us, a basic selfishness and tendency to corruption, which is defined by the old fashioned and very unpopular word 'sin'. I also realised that this was what the Christians I had met had told me and that they claimed they had found the solution to this problem in the person of Jesus Christ. For the next two months a huge battle was going on inside me. I knew in my heart that I could not get away from Jesus, and yet I did not want to become a Christian.

The battle came to a head on New Year's Eve 1969. I spent the last evening of the 1960s at a very decadent and drunken party and woke up the next day with a hangover and a bad conscience and an amazing feeling that I needed to make peace with God. The story of the Prodigal Son, which I remembered from my childhood, came back to me, and I saw myself eating the pig food of my generation and wasting away inside. I felt that God was saying to me, 'Now you have to make a choice – to carry on down the road you are going which will lead to destruction or to turn to me and find the way to life.' I prayed there and then asking God to forgive me for all the wrong things I had done and to change my life.

Almost immediately I felt peace and I knew that I had experienced what Christians call being born again. I went up to Retford and told Alec, one of the boys at the school, what had happened. He told me that they had been praying for me for the past six months at his church. I went along to the church and heard the Pastor speak about how when Jesus died on the cross he took the punishment for our sins and rose again to make it possible for us to come to know God and receive eternal life. New Year's Day 1970, the first day of the new decade, had brought me to a new life.

I decided to see whether prayer worked and so I prayed that I would meet the girl who had given me the leaflet at the demonstration in Grosvenor Square. A couple of weeks later, I went to a meeting in central London and she was there giving her story about how the Lord had brought her out of the Communist Party and told her to go and give out leaflets at demonstrations like the one I had been on. I went and told her how I had received one of her leaflets and now become a Christian, and she was delighted.

Her name was Nikki and we started going out together to Speakers' Corner in Hyde Park and other places in central London to give out leaflets and talk to people about Jesus. We discovered that this was not our only common interest, in fact we realised that we loved each other! So we got married and enjoyed 27 years together until Nikki became ill with multiple myeloma, a cancer of the bone marrow, and died in 1998.

I went along to Bible studies with Nikki and found out that there were people in London too who took this message seriously. Both of us came to the same conclusion about the Bible – that it is not just a dusty old book, but it contains amazing insights into our time. These insights pushed us to a very disturbing, but very exciting conclusion – that the prophecies of the end times are being fulfilled today and that the time of trouble called the Great Tribulation is on its way, which also means that Jesus is coming back. As the world looks to fortune tellers, astrologers, New Age gurus and Nostradamus for their ideas about what is to come, the true source of information vital to our survival in this age and the next is for the most part being ignored. This book is dedicated to those who wish to swim against the tide and look into the source of real enlightenment as to what is going to happen in this world and the next – the Bible!

Chapter 1

So When Will Jesus Come Back?

This is the question everyone wants to know, but the one question we can be sure we will not have the answer to. Jesus said,

> *'But of that day and hour no one knows, no, not even the angels of heaven, but My Father only.'*   (Matthew 24:36)

Paul also wrote about this:

> *'But concerning the times and the seasons, brethren, you have no need that I should write to you. For you yourselves know perfectly that the day of the Lord so comes as a thief in the night. For when they say, "Peace and safety!" then sudden destruction comes upon them, as labour pains upon a pregnant woman.'*   (1 Thessalonians 5:1–3)

Someone once sent me a book with the title *40 reasons why Jesus is coming again in 1988*. The book was not a best seller in 1989. Date setters (especially the Jehovah's Witnesses) have done great harm to this teaching, making it the subject of ridicule when the supposed date of the second coming comes and goes with nothing happening.

In fact if we could work out the date then one of the main points of the teaching would be lost. Suppose we could work out that Jesus is coming back in June 2007. Many people would think, 'Well I can carry on living the way I am until May 2007 and then I'll get ready to meet him.' Because we don't know the date we are to be ready all the time, as John wrote in his letter,

> *'Everyone who has this hope in Him purifies himself, just as He is pure.'*   (1 John 3:3)

In 1 Thessalonians 5:2 the coming of the Lord is compared to the coming of a *'thief in the night'*. The thief does not ring us up to say, 'I'm coming round to rob your house at midnight tomorrow.' Because we know there is always a possibility that a thief could come to rob us, we take precautions all the time to keep our property secure as far as we are able.

If a thief does break in, there are some things he will take and some things he will leave behind. If we leave a £50 note or a gold ring lying around, he will take them. But he will not take our dirty socks or old toothbrush. He takes what has value to him and leaves behind what has no value. Jesus is coming to take what has value to him – those who have accepted him as Saviour – and leave behind those who have not.

Despite the fact that we do not know the exact time of Jesus' return, there are a number of signs he has given us in the Bible of conditions on the earth at the time of his return. When he told the disciples what these were, he said,

> *'When these things **begin** to happen, look up and lift up your heads, because your redemption draws near.'*
>
> (Luke 21:28)

It is interesting that he used the word 'begin' here, because this indicates that when a certain process has begun, you know that it is leading to the final point, in this case the second coming of Jesus. So although the Lord does not want us to waste time trying to work out the date of his return, he does want us to be aware of the signs of his return.

When you approach a great city you get first to the suburbs, and you know that once you get to them if you continue in the same direction you will reach the centre of the city. When you get near a mountain range you come first to the foothills and know that if you keep going you will reach the high mountains. So when you see certain things beginning to happen, you know that the end result is going to be the second coming of Jesus.

Therefore it is important that we can identify the major signs given in the Bible for the second coming. They will become our road map pointing us in the direction of the main event – the glorious return of the Lord Jesus. These are some of the major ones:

1. The Jewish people back in Israel and a time of trouble centring on that land, especially focusing on the status of Jerusalem.

2. Globalisation, causing the emergence of a one-world political system, which will ultimately be controlled by the Antichrist.

3. A falling away from the truth within professing Christendom, leading to a coming together of world religions in a religious system described as the *'whore of Babylon'*.

4. The collapse of moral values and the breakdown of family life bringing with it all kinds of related evils – drug abuse, violence, sexually related diseases, etc.

5. An increase in wars and conflicts within nations, also famines and plagues, causing people to be afraid of what is coming on the earth.

6. A massive invasion of the earth from the demonic realm, causing people to become involved in the occult and to mock and blaspheme the God of the Bible.

7. Dramatic increase in natural disasters as human mismanagement of the planet brings us all to the brink of destruction.

8. Increased scientific knowledge bringing about the technology needed to control the world by the Antichrist.

9. A false peace process which appears to bring a solution to the problems of the world, but in fact leads to a time of trouble unlike any other, which without divine intervention would lead to the end of all life on earth.

10. The message of the Gospel reaching all nations despite opposition and persecution.

In the verses from Paul's letter to the Thessalonians quoted earlier, there is reference to the woman in labour. This is a picture, which is used in both the Old and New Testaments, for the last days of this age. Three observations can be made about the woman in labour. When a woman goes into labour a process begins which cannot be reversed until the child is born. She experiences a series of shocks, known as contractions, which become more intense as she gets nearer to the birth of the child. When the child is born she quickly forgets the sorrows of the labour she has been through for joy at the birth and the new life that has come into the world.

This picture applies very much to the end times in Bible prophecy. The birth of the child corresponds to the main event, the return of the Lord Jesus Christ in power and glory. Then he will bring an end to the present age of sin and wickedness and establish the millennial reign of peace and justice on the earth, which will cause people to forget the former time of trouble. The birth pains of the woman in labour are the sorrows which the world will go through before this event, which will become more and more intense the nearer we get to the end.

Once a woman goes into labour no one can reverse the process, which will ultimately lead to the birth of the child. Similarly, once the labour pains of the last days have been set in motion (and they have!), no religious or political leader is going to be able to reverse them. They may take some positive measures to slow them down or some harmful measures to speed them up, but no one will be able to prevent events moving towards the final conclusion prophesied in the Bible.

The only thing which will stop the catastrophic process now at work in the world, is the second coming of the Lord Jesus. In chapters 2–8 of this book we will look at some of the signs which point us in the direction of this event. Then in chapters 9–12 we will look at how the prophecies indicate that it will all come to an end.

Chapter 2

World Falling Apart

Is the world falling apart or coming together? Or is it doing both at the same time?

The signs of it falling apart are not hard to detect. Half the world's six billion people live on less than £1.50 a day. One billion people have no clean water and 2.4 billion lack access to basic sanitation. In many areas the situation is getting worse. In sub-Saharan Africa the number of people living in poverty has grown from 220 million in 1990 to 300 million in 1998. More than 3 million people die every year from the effects of air pollution and 2.2 million die from contaminated water.

One million children around the world are forced into prostitution every year and the total number of prostituted children could be as high as 10 million. The United Nations has warned that AIDS will kill 70 million people over the next 20 years, with the infection rate in some African countries running at around 40% of the population. Drug use has become epidemic worldwide, bringing crime, addiction and disease to millions.

Throughout most of the world family life is under constant attack with the majority of children in Britain today being born outside of marriage. A government report estimates that one-third of under sixteen-year-old girls are sexually active with the resulting problems of unwanted pregnancies and sexually transmitted diseases. The government's answer is to tell school clinics to hand out condoms and abortion pills to try to cut teenage pregnancies.

More and more areas of Britain today are suffering from crime and violence, which is involving younger and younger people, and threatening to tear apart the very fabric of our society. Official figures show that crime rose by the greatest margin for over a decade in 2001, while the proportion of crimes solved fell to an all time low. 5.2 million offences were committed while only 326,000 offenders were sentenced in courts. A Mori poll released in May 2002 revealed that one in four British school children has committed a crime in the past year. Newspapers report children as young as four getting on the wrong side of the law as parents, teachers and police fight an increasingly losing battle in restraining youth crime.

The media has a great deal to do with the collapsing standards of behaviour worldwide. Much of the 'entertainment' offered by the TV companies has become like an open sewer flowing through people's homes, offering a constant diet of violence, sex and swearing, encouraging us to be voyeurs into other people's misery and degradation. A report by the Broadcasting Standards Commission found that 50 per cent of viewers said they were concerned about the standard of television programmes. Violence was the most commonly mentioned complaint (*The Times* 29th January 2001). The Internet has opened up a new avenue for the most disgusting and degrading pornography imaginable to be sent direct into peoples' homes.

On an international level there are wars and conflicts fuelled by racial and religious hatred engulfing more and more parts of the world. During the 1990s more than one million people, 90% of whom were civilians, were killed in civil wars. In 1995 alone over 41 million people worldwide were displaced, mostly as a result of war or political repression. Even when conflicts are ended, they usually leave behind broken countries where mobs with guns tyrannise the people, and homes, infrastructure and agriculture are destroyed. Most of the weapons used in conflicts in the developing world come from rich countries, which must bear a heavy responsibility for the human misery they cause.

Conflicts between nations now risk the use of weapons of mass destruction. News reports contemplated the possible death of millions of people in May 2002 as nuclear-armed India and Pakistan faced each other over Kashmir. President Bush declared North Korea, Iran and Iraq to be an 'axis of evil' in his January 2002 'State of the Union' speech, on the grounds that these nations are producing chemical, biological, and potentially nuclear, weapons which could be used in the most dangerous regions of the world.

Global terrorism hit the world's consciousness in a big way with the September 11th attacks on America. According to US Deputy Defence Secretary Paul Wolfowitz speaking at a regional security conference in Singapore in June 2002, the prospect of terrorists developing nuclear capabilities is 'more frightening and dangerous' than nuclear proliferation among nation states. He said the concern that 'nuclear weapons or scientists with nuclear expertise could fall into the hands of rogue regimes or terrorist groups is a very, very real one'.

Another issue of global concern is climate change. The Intergovernmental Panel on Climate Change (IPCC), a United Nations organization, predicted possible global warming over the next hundred years of between 2.5 and 10 degrees Fahrenheit (1.4 to 5.8 degrees Celsius). 'In the last thousand years, the overall range is less than 1 degree (Celsius). The kinds of changes we can expect if the IPCC models are correct are considerably greater than anything that modern society has ever experienced. Destructive flooding would occur in some areas, yet drought in other areas. Billions of people who are living at subsistence level could be affected, leading to massive migrations to urban centres. Such movements could be catastrophic,' said Richard Sklar, Professor Emeritus at the University of California, Los Angeles, and an expert in international development. 'Crime, disease, poverty and unemployment would become uncontrollable, and governments could collapse,' he said, leading to regional destabilization (UPI 26 January 2001).

Scientists released a report predicting that British weather would get rapidly warmer and more unstable. Winters will be mild and very wet with frequent flooding, and most of Britain will be snow free. Even the Scottish mountains will have 90% less snow. Summers will be far hotter and drier everywhere. The winter rainfall will cause most problems. Deep depressions with high winds are expected to dump up to 35% more rain on Britain, leading to more frequent flooding. This combined with higher tides and sea levels could cause severe disruption in the south where most of the extra rain is expected. Large areas of eastern England, especially around the Wash and in Essex and Lincolnshire could be permanently lost to the sea. Central London itself could be at risk (*Guardian* 25th April 2002). On the other hand an alternative projection sees the Gulf Stream changing course because of climate change. The result of this would be that Britain and northern Europe would freeze, becoming as cold as Labrador, Canada, which is on the same latitude.

Worldwide the changing weather patterns are creating drought, floods and famines. As I write this in August 2002 there are reports of catastrophic floods in Central Europe, southern Russia, China, India and Bangladesh. There are also reports of disastrous droughts bringing crop failure and devastating forest fires in North America, Australia and parts of southern Africa. Over 1,000 people died in a freak heat wave in India in May 2002 in which temperatures soared to over 120 degrees Fahrenheit. A downpour of giant hailstones, some the size of eggs, killed 15 people and left hospitals overflowing with head-wound victims in central China in July 2002.

The Arctic polar ice cap is shrinking so rapidly due to global warming that ships may be able to navigate the Northwest Passage each summer by 2015, according to a US Navy report (Earthweek.com 18th March 2002). An enormous floating ice shelf in Antarctica collapsed with staggering speed in March 2002 during one of the warmest summers on record there. The piece of ice that broke off was 650 feet thick, with a surface area of 1,250 square miles, and contained about 500 million billion tons of ice. Temperatures in the region are rising at around five times the global average. 'We're seeing a very rapid and profound response by the ice sheet to a warming that's been around for just a few decades,' said Ted Scambos of the National Snow and Ice Data Centre at the University of Colorado. 'Other ice shelves are closer to the breaking point than we previously thought. Break-ups in some other areas, such as the Ross Ice Shelf, could lead to increases in ice flow off the Antarctic and cause sea level to rise' (*Fox News* 19 March 2002).

Natural disasters caused at least 25,000 deaths worldwide in 2001, more than double the previous year. 2001 was a particularly deadly year for earthquakes, with 65 significant quakes worldwide.

I could go on with more and more information to show that almost anything which is threatening to the survival of the planet is on the increase – breakdown of family life, disease, increased lawlessness, violence, crime, terrorism, climate change, environmental disorder, civil wars, conflicts between nations, the threat of weapons of mass destruction. The best efforts of governments around the world are only holding back the effects of these potential disasters, not solving them or reversing them. The worst efforts of governments are pushing us all nearer and nearer to catastrophe.

On this subject we can make two general observations:

1. All these issues tie up with prophecies given in the Bible for the last days.
2. They are all global and international, not limited to one country or region.

In the book of Jeremiah we read that before the Day of the Lord,

> *'Behold, disaster shall go forth*
> *From nation to nation,*
> *And a great whirlwind shall be raised up*
> *From the farthest parts of the earth.'*   (Jeremiah 25:32)

Whether it is drugs, pornography, organised crime, the arms trade or environmental pollution, what we see today is nations exporting evil one to another and creating a global meltdown into chaos.

Jesus said that the days before his second coming would be *'as in the days of Noah'* and *'as in the days of Lot'* (Luke 17:27–28). In the days of Noah we read that:

> '... *the* LORD *saw that the wickedness of man was great in the earth, and that every intent of the thoughts of his heart was only evil continually ... The earth also was corrupt before God and the earth was filled with violence.'*
>
> (Genesis 6:5, 11)

All over the world we see a huge increase in violence at all levels, in the home, in the streets, between communities and between nations. Much of this violence is fuelled by the material people feed their imaginations with – violent films and TV programmes, drugs and rock music or even religious preachers who incite people to hate in the name of God.

In the days of Lot there was extreme sexual immorality in Sodom with open aggressive homosexuality and gang rape being threatened in the account of Lot's escape from that city (Genesis 19). The sexual revolution of our time has not bought the promised liberation from a repressive morality but a neurotic society, obsessed with sex, but unable to show care and love which God intended to be the bedrock of human relationships. Disease, unwanted and unloved children, depression, insecurity and loneliness are just some of the results of the permissive society.

The basic building block of all human society, the family, is being undermined by governments, education and the media. As a result young people become more and more alienated from all authority and out of control. According to Bible prophecy youth in rebellion against their parents and lawlessness will be a feature of the last days (2 Timothy 3:1–5; 2 Thessalonians 2:7). The primary responsibility for this state of affairs is not with the young people, but with the older generation who have abandoned discipline and systematically corrupted the morals of the younger generation.

Much of this is being done by governments themselves as the education systems of the world indoctrinate the young with immoral sex education. The *Washington Times* (10th May 2002) ran an article on a book being passed out at United Nations Child Summit, which encourages children to engage in sexual activities with other minors and with homosexuals. The book is guided by the dominant idea today that there is no absolute right and wrong but we should do what feels right for ourselves. Here is an example of the kind of advice the book gives to the young:

> Sexual relations with a partner: Here we should insist there is no ideal or perfect relations between two or several people. The one that gives us the most satisfaction and that which is adapted to our way of being and the style of life we have chosen. This is why we encounter many differences among women. Some women like to have relations with men. And others with another woman.

God says there is an absolute standard of right and wrong and that he wants us to obey the laws written in the Bible. He says the only acceptable sexual relationship is between a man and a woman who are committed to each other through marriage. Today it is virtually forbidden to say this to young people in schools or on the media, with the result that everyone does what is right in their own eyes. This is not a recipe for freedom but for chaos and ultimately a new kind of tyranny and control system.

The corruption of the young also means that we are heading for God's judgement. Jesus gave a very severe warning about those who corrupt the young:

> *'But whoever causes one of these little ones who believe in Me to sin, it would be better for him if a millstone were hung*

*around his neck, and he were drowned in the depth of the
sea.'*   (Matthew 18:6)

If this were to be applied literally today there would be a
great shortage of millstones.

All these things happening mean that a time of judgement
is coming on the earth as a result of human wickedness. This
time is known as the Great Tribulation and is described in
Jesus' teaching in Matthew 24 and in Revelation 6–19. There
is a way to be saved from the judgement that is coming,
through repenting of sin and believing in Jesus as Saviour and
Lord. We see the signs of the coming Great Tribulation, so the
sensible person will accept the salvation Jesus is offering.

The prophecies indicate that most people will not accept
this offer. In Revelation 9:20–21 we read that at this time
when severe judgements of God are striking the earth,

> *'... the rest of mankind ... did not repent of their murders or
> their sorceries or their sexual immorality or their thefts.'*

Maybe one reason for this is the influence of the media. If
you were to take murder, sorcery (the occult), sexual
immorality and crime out of popular entertainment today
there would not be much left.

Society is being indoctrinated to call good evil and evil
good. People think they have become liberated from old-
fashioned morality, but in fact they are being controlled by a
system which makes huge sums of money from corrupting
others and which is imposing selfishness and immorality
as a way of life to be admired. Sometimes people think they
are being daring rebels against convention by following this
way of life. They are not. They are being the most slavish
conformists.

Jesus also said that in the last days before his return,

> *'Nation will rise against nation, and kingdom against king-
> dom. And there will be famines, pestilences and earthquakes
> in various places.'*   (Matthew 24:7)

The word used for nation is *'ethnos'* from which we have the word 'ethnic'. The implication here is that there will be a huge increase in conflicts within nations caused by racial and religious strife and an increase in conflicts between nations.

There will also be an increase in famines, plagues and earthquakes (natural disasters). Wars, conflicts and bad government are a major reason for famine. Potentially fertile and prosperous countries like Zimbabwe now lie in ruins due to the devastation caused to the agriculture by armed mobs taking over the farms and leaving them untended. Other countries like Angola have had their agriculture ruined by land mines, making the land too dangerous to farm.

Another reason for famine and plague is climate change, which brings with it all kinds of natural disasters. It is remarkable how many aspects of climate change fit in with trends pointed to in Bible prophecies. Jesus said in the days before his second coming there would be a time of *'distress of nations, with perplexity, the sea and the waves roaring; men's hearts failing them from fear and the expectation of those things which are coming on the earth'* (Luke 21:25–26). As a result of climate change there is an increase in storms and the threat of flooding from the sea as levels rise because of the melting of the polar ice.

In Revelation 8:7 we read of one third of the trees being burned up. Today trees are being deliberately burned in the great rain forests of the Amazon and Indonesia for commercial profit. This contributes to global warming, which in turn causes an increase in forest fires and further destruction of tree life around the world. Ola Ullsten, former Swedish Prime Minister and co-chairman of the World Commission on Forests and Sustainable Development said the latest evidence indicates that over half the world's boreal forest could disappear due to the effect of climate change as conditions shift. Boreal, or northern, forests are a belt of mostly coniferous trees running through much of Canada, the United States, Russia, Scandinavia and parts of Mongolia and China. They make up about one-third of the earth's forests.

As a result of forest fires in the USA in the summer of 2002, wild animals have been driven from their homes in desperation at the dried up streams and burning forests and are coming into people's homes in search of food. The situation is just like the description of the end times in the Old Testament prophet Joel:

> *'Alas for that day!*
> *   For the day of the* LORD *is near;*
> *   it will come like destruction from the Almighty.*
> *Has not the food been cut off*
> *   before our very eyes –*
> *   joy and gladness from the house of our God?*
> *The seeds are shrivelled beneath the clods.*
> *The storehouses are in ruins,*
> *   the granaries have been broken down,*
> *   for the grain has dried up.*
> *How the cattle moan!*
> *   The herds mill about*
> *because they have no pasture;*
> *   even the flocks of sheep are suffering.*
> *To you, O* LORD*, I call,*
> *   for fire has devoured the open pastures*
> *   and flames have burned up all the trees*
> *   of the field.*
> *Even the wild animals pant for you;*
> *   the streams of water have dried up*
> *   and fire has devoured the open pastures.'*
>
> (Joel 1:15–20 NIV)

The Indian heat wave and the Chinese hail stones referred to above are a warning of the conditions at the end of the tribulation period when great heat causes men to be scorched and massive hail stones fall on the earth:

> *'Then the fourth angel poured out his bowl on the sun, and power was given to him to scorch men with fire. And men were scorched with great heat.'*   (Revelation 16:8–9)

> *'And great hail from heaven fell upon men, every hailstone about the weight of a talent. And men blasphemed God because of the plague of the hail, since that plague was exceedingly great.'* (Revelation 16:21)

All of these events are a wake up call to the world of the approach of the calamities described in the book of Revelation.

We are not there yet, but to use the image of the previous chapter, we are like the traveller reaching the suburbs of a city who knows that if he carries on in the same direction he will reach the city centre. Today we have reached the outskirts of the city of the Great Tribulation. Current events are pointing inevitably to the final crisis described in the Bible. It is already too late to change direction on most of the issues mentioned in this chapter. When we understand this it is natural that we should feel afraid of the future. Jesus said,

> *'And there will be signs in the sun, in the moon, and in the stars; and on the earth distress of nations, with perplexity, the sea and the waves roaring; men's hearts failing them from fear and the expectation of those things which are coming on the earth, for the powers of heaven will be shaken.'* (Luke 21:25–26)

But God does not want us to collapse in fear. He wants to give us great hope in looking for the second coming of Jesus Christ. Those who believe in Jesus do not have to give way to fear and despair, because there is a glorious hopeful conclusion to all these things which are happening now. Jesus is coming to bring an end to human mismanagement of the planet God gave us to look after and to rescue those who put their trust in him. Then he is going to bring in a glorious new world order in which there will be peace and justice and the earth will be filled with the knowledge of the Lord as the waters cover the sea.

But first there will be a less than glorious new world order, the development of which is intimately related to all the things we have looked at in this chapter.

Chapter 3

World Coming Together

One of the things we noticed in the previous chapter is that all of the things threatening the future of humanity are global issues, not national ones. Logically it follows therefore that the solution to these problems is a global government, not national ones. Is the world moving in this direction?

There is no question that we live in a world that is coming together as never before. As I sit in London writing this book, I can send chapters of it by e-mail to people in New Zealand to read and comment on, as easily or even more easily than I can give it to my next-door neighbour. I can switch on the TV to receive the latest news at any time of the day to check if anything has happened in the world, which affects the issues I am writing about. I can travel to another part of the world in a matter of hours and right to the other side of the world in one day.

What happens in one country affects another. An accounting fraud in a large company in the USA causes stocks to plunge around the world. The threat of war in the Middle East sends the nations into a panic as they fear for the oil supply necessary to keep their economies going. Repressive regimes and conflicts in one part of the world send waves of refugees to seek asylum in another. As international travel, commerce and modern means of communication have shrunk the world into a 'global village', the problems of humanity have also become international ones – drugs, terrorism, climate change, environmental pollution, AIDS, international crime, the arms trade, refugees and asylum.

When Yitzhak Rabin, the Israeli Prime Minister, was assassinated in Tel Aviv in 1995, the news was flashed around the world the moment it happened and within two days the leaders of the world had assembled in Jerusalem for his funeral. Do we ever stop to consider how extraordinary this is? Two hundred years ago it would have taken weeks for the news to get around the world and months to get the leaders to Jerusalem. And they would have had no incentive to go anyway because what happened in Jerusalem would have had little or no interest to them.

Today, because of technology and the way the world is coming together, people know what is going on in countries remote from their own and are affected by such events. The most dramatic example of this was the September 11th attack on New York, which was transmitted live to our TV screens. As pictures of the aircraft crashing into the Twin Towers and the buildings falling were shown around the world, the world was brought together in horror at the event. As a result the USA was able to bring together a global coalition against terrorism.

In the book of Daniel we read that in the end times *'many shall run to and fro and knowledge shall increase'* (Daniel 12:4). Two hundred years ago the fastest anyone could travel anywhere in the world was the speed of a horse. As a result many people hardly ever left the area they were born in. Today we accept car, train and plane travel as a fact of life, with the result that in the developed world most people don't live in the place they were born and don't work in the place where they live. Many people are likely to do business, take holidays and even make friends in places hundreds or thousands of miles from their homes.

The increase in knowledge has caused an explosion of technology, which has totally transformed every aspect of life. Businessmen in London can do deals in Tokyo without leaving their offices, TV journalists can carry instant information of what is happening in Afghanistan into homes in America, people from the Persian Gulf can communicate with people in Australia in Internet chat rooms. You can use the same credit card all over the world to pay your bills.

One of the most interesting developments along these lines is the push towards a cashless society. Credit cards have a great advantage over cash in that they save having to carry around wallets full of notes. If you are crossing from one currency to another you don't have to change your money either. They have a major disadvantage in that someone somewhere knows what you are spending your money on and where you are. If I travel by car from London to Liverpool and fill up with petrol in Liverpool using my credit card, someone knows I have been to Liverpool. If I use cash they don't. In the event of a police state emerging out of our present system this could be used to snoop on people's lives in a way which Hitler or Stalin could only have dreamed of. The other big problem with credit cards is that they can be lost, stolen or swiped so that information from your card can be duplicated onto a forged card, giving the forger the opportunity to spend your money!

With this in mind there are some interesting developments in the pipeline. The Japanese government is assigning each of Japan's 126 million citizens an ID number that will link into a nationwide computer system. The idea is to streamline Japan's bureaucracy by making it easy to obtain basic personal information during administrative procedures. For now, only a person's name, address, gender and date of birth are stored under their ID number. But the government plans that by August 2003 people will receive a card embedded with a computer chip, allowing instant identification.

In America a new product is being developed called Verichip, which involves a microchip implanted beneath the skin, capable of holding the owner's personal identification and medical and bank records. The device is read when a scanner is passed across it.

The newer versions of the VeriChip will hold up to a megabyte of programmable data, and some include a global positioning tracking feature accessible by satellite (i.e. it will give information about where a person is at any time). For this reason it is of great interest to South American business-men afraid of being kidnapped. With the number of children disappearing it would also have attractions as a means of being able to locate any missing child quickly. This would deter abductors who would be afraid of being caught in the act with the help of Verichip.

After the September 11th attacks Richard Sullivan, Director of Applied Digital Solutions, saw the potential for Verichip as a means of improving security: 'Today's security measures don't work very well,' he said and he has a better idea, namely, implant all foreigners passing through customs or immigra-tions with the chips. The implanted chip would replace green cards, 'allowing officials to monitor their activities better and keep terrorists out.' In the wake of September 11th, he said, 'the government is more prepared, for the overall benefit of our citizens, to advocate some of these changes.'

The potential does not stop there. In a report in the Palm Beach Post, Deborah Circelli wrote: 'In five years, Sullivan said he can see the chips being used in children, the elderly, prisoners, and by employers at facilities such as airports and nuclear plants. Society in general could use them instead of ATM or credit cards.'

The possibility of such a device being used instead of credit cards brings this whole issue into focus on our subject of Bible prophecy. In the Book of Revelation we read of a prophecy, which until our time seemed entirely impossible to fulfil. Revelation 13:16–18 describes how the coming Antichrist or beast takes over the world by controlling people's ability to buy and sell:

> *'He causes all, both small and great, rich and poor, free and slave, to receive a mark on their right hand or their foreheads, and that no one may buy or sell except one who has the mark of the beast, or the number of his name. Here is wisdom. Let him who has understanding calculate the number of the beast, for it is the number of a man: His number is 666.'*

With the arrival of Verichip and similar technological developments, the prophecy has become very possible to fulfil. How could John writing the book of Revelation in a society, which used pen and ink to transmit messages and coins to buy and sell, have had any idea about this possible development?

Interestingly Applied Digital Solutions Chief Technology Officer Dr Keith Bolton, has already expressed exasperation over implantation protests coming from a 'noisy 20 percent', whom he identified as Christians who believe the Digital Angel chip is the 'mark of the beast'. He was sure 'the other 80 percent wouldn't mind'.

Apart from Verichip there are several other leaps forward in technology, which have the effect of creating the potential for the population being controlled by a central authority. City centres, motorways and train stations all have video cameras monitoring who is going where and what is going on. If you are out and about you are bound to be caught on camera somewhere. In particular if you go on any sort of protest march or demonstration you will be filmed on video cameras by police or security personnel. Some advanced cameras being used in the USA can now pick out the faces of wanted individuals in a crowd by using facial recognition software to assist police in identifying and catching criminals and missing persons. According to Tom Colatosti, president of Viisage Technology based in Littleton, Massachusetts, the process is so efficient that, 'We can match one face against a database of 8 million images in under 15 seconds.'

Satellite cameras can monitor what is going on from space and beam back information to government agencies. Professor David Begg, chairman of the UK government-sponsored Commission for Integrated Transport, has proposed plans, which will include fitting cars with a black box, which would be tracked by global positioning satellites. Information collected would be fed into a computer, which would charge us for using the roads. In this case whether I use my credit card or not to fill up in Liverpool will make no difference! Someone will know where I am whenever I travel in my car.

A new British produced camera uses an obscure form of radiation called T-rays by which it can see through fog, smoke and even walls and clothing. This could have great benefits in detecting terrorists concealing weapons beneath clothing. It could also be used to survey what people are doing inside their own homes. 'Big Brother is watching you' is already a reality in public places and with this kind of technology it could become a reality in our homes.

Certainly 'Big Brother' already has the ability to listen to you via the Echelon communications monitoring system run by the American 'National Security Agency' based at Morwenstow in Cornwall and Menwith Hills, North Yorkshire. This system monitors telephone, fax and e-mail communications throughout Europe and elsewhere. It is programmed to lock on to a particular communication for analysis if certain 'key' words are used in that conversation. If you carry a mobile phone, it emits a radio signal to the nearest base station. With the co-operation of the mobile phone companies your movements can be tracked.

All this technology makes it quite possible that the kind of dictatorship described in the Bible prophecies for the end times could emerge in our time. So it is important to ask if this fits in with the direction in which current world political developments are heading.

New World Order

In the Middle Ages the feudal system of local lords and barons gave way to national governments and states, as the problems of politics and commerce became too big for the feudal structure to cope with. Today the problems of the world are too big for the individual nations to deal with and a 'new world order' is emerging which claims to have the global scope to deal with these global problems. Therefore we see the nations of the world moving closer together, preparing to surrender sovereignty to growing international power blocs.

In an address to the UN on 7 December 1988 Mikhail

Gorbachev, then President of the Soviet Union, said, 'World progress is only possible through a search for universal human consensus as we move forward to a new world order.' Since the demise of the Soviet Union and his fall from power in Russia, Gorbachev has been active on the world scene, based in the USA, and promoting the need for a world government. The number one reason he cites for this is the environment. He contends that a global institution is needed to deal with this global problem, and if we don't act soon, it will be too late – the world will self-destruct. As part of his push for world government, Gorbachev proposes his 'Earth Charter', a document for which he has become the chief spokesperson and which he believes will save the planet.

Speaking on 11th September 1990 former President Bush said,

> The crisis in the Persian Gulf offers a rare opportunity to move towards a historic period of cooperation. Out of these troubled times a new world order can emerge in which the nations of the world, east and west, north and south, can prosper and live in harmony. Today the new world is struggling to be born.

The idea of a global government is not something which has just emerged as a result of the present world crisis. Back in 1962, Nelson Rockefeller, former Governor of New York, published a book called *The Future of Federalism* in which he claimed that that current events compellingly demand a 'new world order', as the old order is crumbling, and there is 'a new and free order struggling to be born'. Rockefeller says that 'the nation-state is becoming less and less competent to perform its international political tasks. These are some of the reasons pressing us to lead vigorously toward the true building of a new world order'.

On 20 July 1992 *Time* magazine published an article entitled 'The Birth of the Global Nation' by Strobe Talbott, a friend and former room mate at Oxford University of then President Clinton, in which he wrote:

All countries are basically social arrangements. No matter how permanent or even sacred they may seem at any one time, in fact they are all artificial and temporary. Perhaps national sovereignty wasn't such a great idea after all. But it has taken the events in our own wondrous and terrible century to clinch the case for world government.

Talbott was later appointed by Clinton as number two man in the US State Department.

In 1996 The United Nations published a 420-page report *Our Global Neighbourhood* which outlined a plan for 'global governance'. (By 1996 the term 'global governance' had replaced 'New World Order' in such communications.) The UN is the most obvious vehicle to bring in some kind of global government. In December 2001 UN Secretary General, Kofi Annan, gave a speech in Oslo as he received the Nobel Peace Prize on behalf of the UN. He said,

In the 21st Century I believe the mission of the United Nations will be defined by a new, more profound, awareness of the sanctity and dignity of every human life, regardless of race or religion. This will require us to look beyond the framework of states, and beneath the surface of nations or communities.

In other words states, nations and communities are not able to guarantee human dignity. We are now moving beyond the age of government by states and nations into the age of government by blocs of nations, and ultimately to a kind of world government mediated by the UN.

The most successful experiment in this direction in the world today is the European Union. Here we see once powerful nation states like France, Germany, Italy and Spain, pooling their sovereignty and their economies to create the kind of basic building bloc of the global system, which the planners of this experiment have long been working towards. At the time of writing Great Britain remains outside the most important part of that union, the single currency, a situation our present leader, Tony Blair, wishes to change.

Speaking in Warsaw (6th October 2000) Blair unveiled his vision of Europe as the 'next superpower' in terms which line up with the globalist agenda. He said,

> Whatever its origin, Europe today is no longer just about peace. It is about projecting collective power. Europe is a Europe of free, independent, sovereign nations who choose to pool their sovereignty in pursuit of their own interests and the common good.

Professor Anthony Giddens, Director of the London School of Economics and one of Tony Blair's mentors, wrote in *Newsweek* (28th September 1998) that he sees the EU 'as a pioneering phenomenon; not a nation-state, not a federation, but something different, an attempt to provide a political form for a globalised world'.

Despite all its faults, the EU has become a model for other regions of the world. After the launch of the Euro, *The Times* (27th January 1999) contained an article saying:

> The Euro may have only been in existence for less than a month and been entirely untested as a concept, but its arrival has given birth to a new mania for monetary unions. Asia is talking about an Asian single currency. Economics professors from Vancouver and Toronto are advocating a single North American currency as the logical next step to the NAFTA free trade area. The idea of monetary union between Australia and New Zealand has been mooted. Some go even further advocating a world monetary union: a single, single currency.

The article concludes that a single world currency would need a world government, something it considers a very remote possibility.

Perhaps not so remote. Three years on from this Gary Kah,

a Christian researcher into the development of globalism, wrote in his May 2002 newsletter,

> For all practical purposes the world is now down to two major currencies – the US Dollar and the Euro. Most international trade in the immediate future will be conducted in one of these denominations. A distant second (for a time) will be the British Pound, the Swiss Franc and the Japanese Yen. But I believe these too will eventually yield to the Dollar and the Euro, and ultimately to a single global currency (or electronic unit of exchange).

Other regions of the world are pushing for integration along the lines of the EU. In October 2001 the oil rich Gulf States announced that they were working towards monetary union and a single currency in an effort to forge a strong Arabian Peninsula economic bloc able to exert influence on the world stage.

In June 2002 the first summit of the African Union (AU) opened in Durban, South Africa. The union, loosely modelled on the European Union, proposes to create an African peace and security council able to send in peace-keepers to halt wars, an African parliament, a common court of justice, a central bank, and eventually a single currency.

In July 2002 South Korean economists issued a call to create a common currency in Asia, similar to the Euro. Choi Gong-pil, researcher at the Korea Institute of Finance advocated 'the establishment of an independent regional capital market in Asia and its single currency' bringing together the four major Asian countries, South Korea, Japan, China and Taiwan.

The EU is aspiring to a position of leadership in putting the world to rights. European Commissioner in charge of trade, Pascal Lamy, has called for a new world order to solve the globalisation problems. In a speech on 6th May 2002, he called for the EU to speak through a 'single mouth' at global level and to 'assume a stronger role in the world to achieve a more equitable global order'.

At a summit in Rome on 21st May 2002, something unthinkable twenty years ago took place, as Russia signed an agreement establishing a joint council to work with NATO on a range of issues that Italian Prime Minister Berlusconi said represented the end of the Cold War. The transformation of Russia from the Communist enemy into a partner with the west in the search for global security is an enormous step forward in the direction of world government. Berlusconi went further stating the view that Europe with its central position between the former super-power rivals is well situated to become the global kingpin. 'I believe that with Russia as a member of Europe, Europe will become the world's primary political centre – with an alliance with the United States,' he said.

As Europe seeks to increase its influence in the world many European politicians are saying there needs to be a recognisable European President. On 15th May 2002 France and Britain joined forces to demand the creation of a such a figure who, according to Tony Blair, will become the public face and driving force of Europe. The goal is to give Europe a high-profile political leader, who would also serve as the European Union's face in international affairs and take a key role in developing defence and foreign policies. They believe the new president would give the European Union a sharper identity, providing much-needed leadership and accountability. Are all these developments political matters with no relevance to the Bible, or do they tie in with prophecies in a way which is vital for us to understand?

Chapter 4

New Europe, Old Danger

Out of Europe came the Roman Empire, ruling much of the continent and the Mediterranean area, including Israel at the time of Jesus Christ. The Christian Church began its history in the days of the Roman Empire, first fiercely persecuted by it and ultimately embraced by it in 312 when Constantine became Emperor. When Christianity became the official religion of the Roman Empire, many true Christians saw this not as a triumph, but a disaster for the faith, as a corrupted, paganised form of Christianity began to rule over much of Europe. As a result Christianity changed from being a persecuted faith, which people adopted generally because they believed its message, into the dominant faith, largely made up of unbelievers who changed their labels, but not their nature. Practices which had no basis at all in the New Testament were introduced, corrupting the Church from within.

Major errors concerning the Christian faith were introduced, which developed into the religious system known as Roman Catholicism. (See Appendix 2 for further information on this subject.) The liberating truth of the Gospel was replaced with a system which bound people up with dead works in the vain attempt to earn salvation and brought them into submission to a corrupted clergy. In the minds of most people Christianity became identified with this religion, a fact which causes many people today to reject the faith.

From the time of the conversion of Constantine onwards the power of the Bishop of Rome grew, as this post developed into the Papacy. When the Roman Empire fell in 476, the Pope began to take on the role of the Roman Emperor, even using one of his titles, 'Pontifex Maximus', or Pontiff, which means 'Supreme Bridge Maker'. When applied to the Emperor it meant on one level the guardian of the bridges over the Tiber River leading into Rome, but on another level it gave divine status to the Emperor claiming that he was the bridge connecting this life and the next.

When applied to the Pope it meant that he became 'Vicarius Filii Dei' the Vicar (or one in place of) the Son of God and took on an increasingly divine status. This concept led to the doctrine of the infallibility of the Pope and of the Church he led. The Catholic Catechism states that the Pope is infallible, with this definition of what it means:

> When I say that the Pope is infallible, I mean that the Pope cannot err when, as Shepherd and Teacher of all Christians, he defines a doctrine concerning faith or morals, to be held by the whole church.   (Article 93)

The Catechism goes on to say that:

> the Church cannot err in what she teaches as to faith or morals, for she is our infallible guide in both.
>
> (Article 100)

In fact by the Middle Ages the lives of Popes had become a public scandal as they amassed enormous wealth, and lived lives of gross corruption and vice. The Catholic Church became a source of oppression and violence through the Crusades and Inquisition, which massacred Jews, Muslims and dissenting Christians (who were mostly true believers in Jesus).

It is interesting to visit the 'Palace of the Popes' in Avignon, France, where the medieval popes set up their headquarters in the 13th century due to trouble in Rome. In one of the halls called the Curia you can see the letters SPQR (Senatus Populus Que Romanus, the seal of the Roman Empire) on the wall, which according to the official guide shows that the Papacy continued the governing role of the Roman Empire in Europe.

A study of history shows how this is the case. In AD 800 Charlemagne (Charles the Great), a zealous Roman Catholic, was crowned 'Imperator Romanorum' (Emperor of the Romans) by Pope Leo III. He became Western Europe's 'Christian' Caesar – a Roman Emperor born of a Germanic race, ruling over the 'Holy Roman Empire'. He was proclaimed 'Rex Pater Europae' (King Father of Europe) and wanted to create a unified Catholic Europe, which would be 'Christianised' at sword point, in alliance with the Pope.

After centuries of schisms and conflicts the imperial crown was given to the Austrian, Count Rudolph of Habsburg. During the 15th and 16th centuries the imperial title became hereditary in the Habsburg family. The greatest of all the Habsburgs, the Emperor Charles V, built an empire stretching from Vienna to Peru through the acquisition of Spanish dominions and again pursued the ideal of a unified Catholic Empire. The Protestant Reformation was a major feature in bringing an end to this attempt to unify Europe under Rome.

Napoleon too dreamed of a resurrected Roman-European civilisation, this time dominated by France. At the height of his power he wrote to the Pope: 'Tell the Pope I am Charlemagne, the Sword of the Church, his Emperor, and as such I expect to be treated.' His plans for a United States of Europe came to an end with his defeat by Britain and her allies at Waterloo. From his exile on the island of St Helena he wrote: 'I wanted to found a European system, a European code of laws, a European judiciary. There would have been but one people throughout Europe.'

Mussolini signed a concordat with the Pope and in 1936 declared the resurrection of the Roman Empire through his Italian fascist regime, claiming succession to imperial Rome. The old alliance between Rome and Germany was revived as

Mussolini made a pact with Hitler, whose ambition was to be ruler of a great German Empire uniting Europe under the 1,000-year Reich of Nazi barbarism. During the war the Vatican made virtually no protest at the appalling crimes being committed by the Fascists in Europe.

The coming together of the European Union is the next stage in the remarkable history of reviving the Roman Empire. After the Second World War, Germany and much of Europe lay in ruins. The United States and the Soviet Union emerged as the dominant superpowers, effectively dividing Germany and Europe between them in terms of influence.

Today the Soviet Union is no more and although America remains the most powerful nation on earth at the moment, there are those in Europe, Tony Blair amongst them, who see Europe as the next superpower. From the small beginnings of the European Coal and Steel Community in 1956, the European Union already has most of the trappings of a super state with ever more power being centralised in its institutions.

The fall of the Communist regimes in Eastern Europe in the late 1980s caused the reunification of Germany and allowed Eastern European countries to come out of Russia's control into the orbit of the European Union. The dominant religion of most countries of the European Union is Roman Catholicism, which played a major part in bringing about the fall of Communism in Eastern Europe, especially in Poland.

When visiting Austria in 1983 Pope John Paul II called for a united Europe, saying, 'Europeans should overcome the menacing international confrontations of states and alliances and create a new united Europe from the Atlantic to the Urals.' Addressing the European Parliament in a symposium on 'Remembering the Origins of the Process of European Integration' in September 1997, Cardinal Martini of Milan outlined the importance of a single faith (Catholicism) and emphasised that religions must not support nationalisms (i.e. the Church of England must not defend the English Constitution), and Europe must recognise the 'primacy of the divine' (i.e. the primacy of the Pope). He said, 'The Europe we must build is a Europe of the spirit,' and reminded the Parliament, 'If the process of European integration is not anchored in truly religious foundations it will seriously compromise the future of all Europeans.' (Information from *The Principality and Power of Europe* by Adrian Hilton.)

The United Kingdom has long been a centre of resistance to Roman Catholic power in Europe, but is little by little capitulating to Catholic domination. Our Prime Minister, Tony Blair, is a Catholic sympathiser and both Conservative and Liberal Parties are now led by Roman Catholics. The Act of Succession forbidding the monarch to marry a Roman Catholic is almost certain to be revoked and the Roman Catholic Church plays an equal role with the Church of England in state functions now. The next Archbishop of Canterbury, Dr Rowan Williams, is highly ecumenical in his outlook and is likely to lead the Church of England into closer association with Rome.

Much of the push towards European integration is in the name of peace and security. The 2002 International Charlemagne Prize that is awarded for contributions to European unity was won by the Euro currency. Wim Duisenberg, the head of the European Central Bank, accepted the award on behalf of the people of the Euro zone. In his acceptance speech he said, 'The vision of a united Europe was born out of a longing for peace and prosperity on a continent that not only was torn apart all too often by internal conflicts but also pulled the rest of the world into two wars.'

Despite the ideals of creating peace and prosperity there is increasing concern at the powers being accumulated by the unelected officials who run the European Commission. Many people see this as a potential dictatorship, endlessly churning out rules which tie up almost every area of human activity in paperwork and bureaucracy. At the same time the 'Human Rights' legislation of the European Union makes it more and more difficult to prosecute criminals and enforce justice, creating a situation in which law-abiding citizens are penalised and oppressed, while criminals are more than likely to get away with their crimes.

The European Court of Justice ruled on 6th March 2001 that the European Union could lawfully suppress political criticism of its institutions and of leading figures, sweeping aside English Common Law and 50 years of European precedents on civil liberties. The EU's top court found that the European Commission was justified in sacking Bernard Connolly, a British economist dismissed in 1995 for writing a book entitled *The Rotten Heart of Europe*. The court was particularly offended at Connolly's suggestion that the Euro project is a threat to democracy, freedom and 'ultimately peace'.

The ruling stated that the commission could restrict dissent in order to 'protect the rights of others' and punish individuals who 'damaged the institution's image and reputation'. This gives the potential to remove the right to dissent and is a pointer to the EU becoming a dictatorship punishing its critics and demanding subservience from its population.

Under the new anti-terrorism measures being introduced in Europe and America following the September 11th attacks, powers are being given to governments to investigate and suppress organisations which threaten the security of the state. This could be applied to legitimate protest groups as well as real terrorists. With this in mind it is disturbing to read that former French Prime Minister, Lionel Jospin, stated that the proposed European army 'will be able to maintain **internal security** as well as prevent conflicts throughout the world.' This means that the European army could be used to crack down on dissenters within the EU as well as defending the EU from would be aggressors.

On 13th April 2000 The European Parliament approved the Dimitrakopoulos-Leinen Report, article 6 of which makes provision for the setting up of EU wide political parties. The report also stated that 'parties that do not respect human rights and democratic principles as set out in the Treaty of Rome shall be the subject of suspension proceedings in the European Court of Justice'.

The catch here is that the whole purpose of the Treaty of Rome is to further European integration with or without the democratic consent of the people. Historically it can be shown that many of the moves towards European integration have not been endorsed by democratic votes in favour of this, but imposed by the elite who control the European Commission. European countries did not have a democratic vote to decide whether they wanted to adopt the Euro currency.

The possibility therefore exists that any party opposed to EU integration could be suspended according to this report. The banning of political parties is a dangerous road to go down in a democracy. It is worth noting that the Soviet Union never abolished elections. The ruling Communist party simply outlawed all other parties as 'fascist' or 'counter revolutionary' and maintained itself in power that way! In many ways we are already half way there, since political parties, which are critical of the EU, are consistently ridiculed and marginalized in the media, which means they have little or no chance of achieving any position of power to influence events.

What is the significance of this?

The prophecies of Daniel and Revelation have many indications that at the end of this age there will be a revival of the Roman Empire which will bring to power the final world ruler, known as the Antichrist or the Beast. Chapters 2 and 7 of Daniel are parallel passages in which God gives insight into the world empires which would follow the Babylonian Empire, which was dominant at the time of Daniel. The fourth empire (Rome) would exist in some form until the second coming of Christ and play a leading role in the last days of this age.

In Daniel 2 Nebuchadnezzar, king of Babylon, had a dream of a great image with a head of gold, chest and arms of silver, legs of iron and feet partly of iron and partly of clay. The image was struck on the feet with a *'stone cut without hands'* and broken in pieces. The stone then became a *'great mountain and filled the whole earth'*, a picture of the second coming of Jesus Christ and the kingdom he will set up on the earth after his return.

In Chapter 7 Daniel himself had a vision of four great

beasts: a lion, a bear, a leopard and *'a fourth beast dreadful and exceedingly strong'*. In Daniel's vision the empires would be overthrown by *'One like the Son of Man, coming with the clouds of heaven'* who would then have an everlasting dominion over *'all peoples, nations and languages'* (Daniel 7:13–14). Jesus quoted this passage, applying it to his second coming in Matthew 24:30 and 26:64.

The interpretation of both chapters is that they refer to a succession of empires, the Babylonian, the Medo-Persian, the Greek and the Roman. All these empires would be run by an oppressive political system, which would be under the spiritual power of *'Mystery Babylon the Great'* (Revelation 17:5) and would therefore conflict in some way with the people of God. The fourth beast (Rome) would be different from all the others in that it would continue in some form until the end of this age and the second coming.

Daniel prophesied that there would arise from *'this kingdom'* (i.e. the Roman Empire), an entity which would be connected to it, but different from it (Daniel 7:24). As we have seen, the Papacy came out of the Roman Empire and continued to concentrate power over Europe in the city of Rome, after the Empire fell in 476. Daniel prophesies that out of this kingdom would come a leader who is described as a *'little horn ... speaking pompous words'* (Daniel 7:8), *'a stern faced king who understands sinister schemes'* (Daniel 8:23) and *'the prince who is to come'* (Daniel 9:26). This one will persecute *'the saints of the Most High'* (Daniel 7:25) and will also make some kind of covenant/treaty with many in Israel for *'one week'* (seven years), a covenant which he will break half way through (Daniel 9:27).

His identity is further revealed in the New Testament book of Revelation where he is called the beast, who persecutes the saints and brings in the *'abomination of desolation'* (Daniel 11:31; Matthew 24:15–31; Revelation 13). The Book of Revelation, written in the days of the persecution of Christianity by the Roman Empire (Daniel's fourth beast), describes a future beast, whose leader will be given power by *'ten kings'* (Revelation 17:10–13). He will make use of a religious system known as *'Mystery Babylon'* to gain world power, but will end up double-crossing this religious union and destroying it (Revelation 17:1–6, 16–18). His rule will be shattered by the Second Coming of Jesus in power and glory at the end of this age.

We saw above that this one would be given power by *'ten kings'*. These kings are spoken of in Daniel 7:24 and in Revelation 17:12–13 where we read:

> *'And the ten horns which you saw are ten kings who have received no kingdom as yet, but they receive authority for one hour as kings with the beast. These are of one mind, and they will give their power and authority to the beast.'*

At the time of writing the Book of Revelation the ten kings had *'received no kingdom as yet'*, in other words they were not contemporary with John who wrote it, but they will be contemporary with the Beast (Antichrist) and will give their power to him. Their time of power will be short lived (one hour – i.e. a short period, not a long period of centuries). When I first became interested in this subject back in the 1970s the general view I picked up from prophetic books was that these kings were ten European nations who would give their power to the Antichrist. However that view seems hard to reconcile with the present enlarged European Union and also raises the question, 'Why should such a leader have worldwide dominion?' as is indicated by Revelation 13.

Gary Kah, whom I have already quoted in the previous chapter, has written a book *World Government: How Close Is It?*. In this he writes about 'The World Constitution and Parliament Association', an umbrella organisation for various religious and political one world organisations, which 'has divided the world into 10 administrative regions upon which the world government will be based. These regions are referred to by insiders as the 10 kingdoms. A total of 5 world capitals are being proposed by the association. Four of these cities would be dubbed secondary world capitals, while one city would be designated the principal world capital.'

The 'Club of Rome' also produced a study back in 1972 in which it said, 'The world cannot be viewed as a uniform whole, but must instead be seen as consisting of distinct though disconnected regions. In our study the world system is divided into ten regions.'

In the previous chapter we also saw how different regions of the world are seeking to create regional blocs with single currencies along the lines of the European Union. The phenomenon of nations coming together is not just a European one and the end result of all this is that national governments become subservient to the central organisation they are merging with. Once you unite currencies, you have to unite the process of government. This process is accelerating in Europe and on current trends will soon reach the point where all major decisions are made by the central European administration, not by the elected governments of individual countries. As Europe comes together there is a call to create a European President and for Europe to play a leading role in world affairs, including the search for a Middle East peace settlement.

Many people today are longing for a strong leader to come to save the world from its present confusion. Could it be that the coming together of the European Union will throw up such a leader? The end time scriptures indicate that in the days immediately before the Second Coming of Christ, a powerful world leader will emerge, promising peace and safety and reviving in some form the old Roman Empire.

It is quite probable that such a one is right now waiting in the wings to appear centre stage and offer a solution to the problems of the world. Some people say this leader will be the next Pope and from certain things indicated in this chapter that would seem to be a possibility. However for reasons which will emerge in the following chapters, my understanding is that he will be a political leader who will be backed by religious leaders. He will come in not like Hitler as a man of war, but as a man of peace and will initially be hailed by many as the Messiah for our time.

Chapter 5

Wanted – a New Religion for the New Age

It is not just political figures who are looking for a new world order in which nation states give way to a global government. Teilhard de Chardin, a controversial Roman Catholic priest, wrote: 'The Age of Nations is past: the task now, if we would not perish, is to build the earth.' In fact a significant driving force for world unity comes from religious as well as political leaders. The name of the game is unity to save the world and create world peace and justice.

The logic then goes that if you are opposed to this unity you must be opposed to peace and justice. This puts pressure on Christians, who should be on the side of peace and justice, to support the process. However when we analyse this way of thinking we discover that there is a new spirituality behind it all, which conflicts with Christianity. Sometimes these ideas are lumped together as 'New Age', but this definition is not always easy to pin down. Generally the main traits are a belief that all roads lead to God, that we need to get in touch with our inner selves, and that there are no absolute values of right and wrong.

Another common idea is that humanity is facing a new crisis, so we need a new 'Christ' or Messiah to come and save us. You will find this idea in many new religious movements

51

as well as in films and TV programmes, which are subtly influencing people to look for a new Messiah figure, while at the same time ridiculing and rejecting anything to do with Jesus Christ and those who follow him.

What is on offer is not to be found in Jesus the Saviour coming from heaven to redeem us, but by discovering the 'god' inside ourselves. Indian guru Swami Muktananda said, 'The only way out is in. Kneel to your own self. Honour and worship your own being. God dwells within you as You.'

Marilyn Ferguson wrote in *Yoga Journal*, July 1981:

> The myth of the saviour 'out there' is being replaced by the myth of the hero 'in here'. Its ultimate expression is the discovery of the divinity within us. In a very real sense we are each other.

To make this discovery people are encouraged to use yoga, meditation, bodily disciplines, encounter groups, and even drugs, occult practices and shamanism.

Many people are in fact unaware of how close much of this comes to straight witchcraft, as Miriam Starhawk wrote in *Yoga Journal*, May 1986:

> Witchcraft is a religion. To reclaim the word 'witch' is to reclaim our right to know the life spirit within as divine. The longing for expanded consciousness has taken many of us on a spiritual journey to the East and to Hindu, Taoist and Buddhist concepts. Eastern religions offer a radically different approach to spirituality than Judeo-Christian traditions. Their goal is not to know God but to be God. In many ways these philosophies are close to that of witchcraft.

In this way of thinking Jesus is considered a great teacher, a possible Messiah for his time, but not the Messiah for all time. Helen Shuchman summed up this view in her *Course in Miracles*:

> Jesus was an historical person, but the Christ is an eternal transpersonal condition.

In plain English this means that the 'Christ' (Messiah) spirit came upon the historical person called Jesus for a time, but then left him. It comes upon different people at different times in history. Therefore there are other religious leaders like Buddha and Mohammed who are equally 'Christ' figures.

In April 1982 the Tara Centre, a New Age group, publicised the coming of a the 'Christ' through full page newspaper advertisements in many countries:

> The Christ is now here pointing the way out of our present crisis. He comes not to judge but to aid and inspire – the World Teacher, Lord Maitreya, known by Christians as the Christ. And as Christians await the Second Coming, so Jews await the Messiah, the Buddhists the fifth Buddha, the Muslims the Imam Mahdi and the Hindus await Krishna. These are names for one individual. His presence in the world guarantees there will be no third world war. With his help we will build a new world.

The New Age agenda is looking to unite all humanity in a new spiritual consciousness. Vera Adler wrote:

> There is actually a Plan and a Purpose behind all creation. World unity is the goal towards which evolution is moving. The world plan includes: A World Organization, a World Economy, a World Religion.
> *(When Humanity Comes of Age*, pp. 190–193)

Some are looking to the UN as the means which will achieve this world union. Sri Chinmoy, Hindu mediator and chaplain at the UN, has said:

> The United Nations is the way, the way of oneness, that leads us to the Supreme Oneness. It is like a river flowing

towards the source, the Ultimate source. The United
Nations becomes for us the answer to world suffering,
world darkness and world ignorance. A day will dawn
when the vision of the United Nations will save the
world.

Robert Muller, a former Assistant General Secretary of the
UN, was profoundly influenced by New Age mysticism and
wrote concerning the UN:

And God saw that all the nations of the earth, black and
white, rich and poor, from north or south, from east and
west and of all creeds were sending their emissaries to a
tall glass house on the shores of the River of the Rising
Sun, on the island of Manhattan (i.e. the UN headquarters in New York), to stand together, to think
together and to care together for all the world and all
its people. And God said: 'That is good.' And it was the
first day of the New Age of the Earth.

(*The Desire to be Human*)

According to Muller, the altar in the UN Meditation
Room is 'dedicated to the god whom man worships under
many names and in many forms.' Behind all of this is
the pantheistic view that god is in everything, the trees, the
earth, the animals, you and me, and that everything is one
inter-connected whole. When we can discover our 'inter-
connectedness' and tap into the power within, we can release
the energies needed to save the world.

This radically opposes biblical Christianity, which teaches
that God is separate from his creation and that he can only
be known through repentance and faith in the Lord Jesus
Christ, who came once in fulfilment of prophecy in order to
die as a sacrifice for sin and rise again from the dead and who
is coming again at the end of this age to judge the world in
righteousness.

Biblical Christianity finds itself under fire not just from the
world but also from much of the Church itself. An article in

the *Daily Telegraph* (31st July 2002) stated that one third of Church of England clergy disbelieve in the resurrection of Jesus and only half are convinced of the truth of the Virgin Birth and that Jesus is the only way to God. Faith in the resurrection of Jesus is vital to Christianity, as Paul wrote in Romans 10:9:

> *'If you confess with your mouth the Lord Jesus and believe in your heart that God has raised him from the dead, you will be saved.'*

Therefore by definition at least one third of the clergy who lead churches in the Church of England are unbelievers!

Much of the visible Church is embracing the inter-faith view that all religions are one and it does not matter what you believe, as long as you are sincere. The Church of England put a prayer on its official website for All Saints Day 2001. The prayer begins by remembering 'the saints in the security of our hearts ... these great women and men of God' who are 'the ancient foundation of our faith and our inspiration'. It continues:

> The saints were not those who were perfect. They were parts of God's creation who struggled and often failed and yet managed to raise up our faith in God and in one another. Abraham, Isaac, Joseph, Sarah, Hannah, Joshua, David, Moses, Mary the Mother of Jesus, **Buddha and Mohammed** and all the prophets of old. They led God's people to God's light.

To include Buddha and Mohammed, whose messages conflict strongly with the message of the Bible, in a list of prophets who 'led God's people to God's light' shows an astonishing departure from the faith handed down by the early Church.

In 1986 the Pope gathered 130 leaders of the world's twelve major religions at Assisi to pray for peace. Praying together were snake worshippers, fire worshippers, spiritists, animists,

North American witch doctors, Buddhists, Muslims, Hindus as well as all denominations of Christians. The Pope declared that all were **'praying to the same God'**. On that occasion the Pope allowed his good friend the Dalai Lama to replace the cross with Buddha on the altar of St Peter's Church in Assisi and for him and his monks to perform their Buddhist worship there. The church was later severely damaged in an earthquake.

Out of the 1986 Assisi event an annual meeting of the world's religious leaders has been inaugurated, led by the Roman Catholic Church. At the meeting held in Barcelona in 2001, Mario Marazziti, spokesman of Rome's Sant Egidio Community, an organizer of the meeting, explained at the opening session:

> Unending wars, nationalist ethnic temptations, and the fear of dialogue – given this panorama, it is a historic occasion that religions meet and together say: 'This third millennium must be characterized by dialogue; dialogue is our planet's need in this phase of globalisation.' And the initiative comes from the heart of the Catholic Church.

Marazitti is here affirming that inter-faith dialogue is a vital building block of the globalisation process. This means that there is a connection between what is going on in the political world and what is going on in the religious world. Commenting on this process, Dave Hunt wrote in his book *A Woman Rides the Beast*:

> Roman Catholicism is proving to be the bridge that brings together all faiths. That fact alone is not surprising, but it is astonishing to see evangelical Christians stepping onto the bridge on one end while at the same time Hindus, Buddhists and pagans of every stripe are stepping onto it from the other. If we are indeed in the last days, as seems apparent, it will not be long until all sides meet in the middle.

As the world religions come together it is clear that the spirit behind this movement is strongly opposed to the biblical concept that there is one God and one way of salvation through repentance and faith in Jesus as Lord. In the speech already quoted in Chapter 3 UN Secretary General Kofi Annan told the audience at the ceremony for receiving the Nobel Prize in Oslo in December 2001:

> The idea that there is one people in possession of the truth, one answer to the world's ills, or one solution to humanity's needs, has done untold harm throughout history – especially in the last century. Today, however, even amidst continuing ethnic conflict around the world, there is a growing understanding that human diversity is both the reality that makes dialogue necessary, and the very basis for that dialogue.

In other words the idea that all religions are equal is the basic building block of the global community that is emerging. To go against it is to be a danger to humanity.

He went on:

> In every great faith and tradition one can find the values of tolerance and mutual understanding. The Quran, for example, tells us that 'We created you from a single pair of male and female and made you into nations and tribes, that you may know each other.' Confucius urged his followers: 'When the good way prevails in the state, speak boldly and act boldly. When the state has lost the way, act boldly and speak softly.' In the Jewish tradition, the injunction to 'love thy neighbour as thyself,' is considered to be the very essence of the Torah. This thought is reflected in the Christian Gospel, which also teaches us to love our enemies and pray for those who wish to persecute us. Hindus are taught that 'truth is one, the sages give it various names.' And in the Buddhist tradition, individuals are urged to act with compassion in every facet of life.

Behind the smooth words of love and tolerance there is an agenda, which is saying:

> There are some people who are opposing the process of global integration and who are a destructive influence on the world. There are Muslims who want to impose Islam by force on the rest of the world. There are Christians who believe the Bible is true and teach that salvation and eternal life only come through Jesus. These people have done great harm to the world and need to be opposed. All gods are equal and those who deny this are not true to their own faith.
>
> (author's interpretation)

The creed of the modern world is really to be found in the Hindu saying 'truth is one and the sages give it various names.' In other words it makes no difference what you believe and who or what you worship, because all religions and philosophies are different expressions of the same thing.

However in the Bible God says,

> 'I am the LORD
>   and there is no other ...
> Ignorant are those who carry about idols of wood,
>   who pray to gods that cannot save ...
>   ... there is no God apart from me,
> a righteous God and a Saviour.'   (Isaiah 45:18–21 NIV)

In other words there is one God, the God revealed in the Bible, who does save, but all other gods do not save.

Jesus said,

> 'I am the way, the truth and the life. No one comes to the Father except through me.'   (John 14:6)

Again this means that Jesus is the way to the Father, but other gods or religious leaders are not. Therefore those who take the Bible seriously cannot agree that all gods are equal.

There is only one God and the only way to know salvation is through faith in Jesus the Messiah. It follows that those who believe this will want to tell non-Christians that they need to believe in Jesus in order to have eternal salvation. If you express this view in public today you will soon find a multitude of people, especially religious leaders, coming down on you like a ton of bricks. It is probably the most politically incorrect view you can hold!

In response to Kofi Annan's speech, Gunnar Berge, Chairman of the Norwegian Nobel Committee, said,

> The idea that mankind has common interests, and that this should find expression in some form or other of shared government or rules, can be traced back to the Roman Empire.

It is very interesting that he refers to the Roman Empire as the basis for some kind of 'shared government'. As we have seen in the last chapter, students of prophecy have long held the view that in the last days before the return of Jesus there will be a revival of the Roman Empire. Although we have seen there is a geographical fulfilment of this in the coming together of the European Union, there is a further spiritual significance in the proposed 'shared government' of the United Nations. In this case the ultimate agenda goes far beyond a revived Roman Empire in Europe and looks to the establishment of a world government backed by a world religion.

It is fascinating to note how what is happening in the spiritual dimension today ties up with what happened in the days of the Roman Empire. Often we have the impression from films like *Ben Hur* of the Roman Empire as brutally suppressing all people it conquered and crushing their ideas and beliefs. But in fact Rome was generally tolerant as far as different religions were concerned, as long as they were registered as 'religio licita' (a legal religion). Legal religions placed their gods in the Pantheon, a building in Rome, which means 'all gods'. They were required to give allegiance to

Caesar but as long as they did this they could practise their religion how they liked.

As well as accepting the supremacy of the Caesar, religions were expected to keep the 'Pax Romana', Roman peace. None of them should disturb this peace by challenging the power of Rome or by stirring up religious or nationalistic conflict. For many people this was a good thing as it stopped warring tribes fighting each other and created a framework of law and order, which brought stability as long as they kept the rules.

The early Christians became a *'religio illicita'* (illegal religion) because they refused to accept the divinity of the Caesar or acknowledge him as 'Lord', since they believed Jesus was Lord. They also were seen as a threat to the peace because they proclaimed the Gospel message to all other faiths, saying that Jesus is the only Saviour and the Messiah. The book of Acts records an incident in Ephesus where a riot took place because of Paul's preaching that images made to the goddess Diana were useless. This was damaging the trade of silversmiths in the city (Acts 19:23–41).

Today in Britain there have been a number of recent cases whereby Christians preaching in the open air have stirred up opposition from people of other faiths, or from homosexuals, and been attacked by them. The Christians have then been charged by the police for disturbing the peace. This is similar to the kind of problems the early Christians faced in the Roman Empire.

The whole emphasis on inter faith dialogue and the equality of all religions is also very similar to the approach to religion in the Roman system. Today all religions are accepted as equal and brought into the modern 'Pantheon' of the inter-faith movement. As yet we do not see a visible 'Caesar' figure, but many are looking for such a figure to arise.

The push towards inter-faith unity in the name of peace is being promoted by the media, the education system and the globalist forces in the religious and political world. It is also preparing the way for the suppression of authentic

Christianity in all countries including traditionally Christian ones. Europe, under influence from Rome, is leading the way in this.

Plans for registration and regulation of religious and 'faith groups' were discussed at a conference held in The Hague on 24th–25th June 2001. Groups which are not registered would be classed as cults or sects, regarded with deep suspicion by the population and discriminated against legally and financially. A report prepared for the French Assembly by the anti-sect commission presided over by Alain Gest served as a reference point for this discussion. It said that 'ecumenism could be the criteria for distinguishing churches from cult groups'. In other words an acceptable church must be ecumenical (and also presumably accept the inter-faith view that all gods are equal). In this case the EU is moving in exactly the same direction as the Roman Empire did as far as religion is concerned.

True Christians cannot enter into this union because we know that Jesus is unique, not to be put on the same level as the founders of other faiths. He is unique because he is God, and he fulfilled the prophecies of the Messiah in the Hebrew Scriptures by laying down his life as a sacrifice for our sins and rising again from the dead. Buddha, Mohammed and even Moses are all dead and buried, but Jesus is unique in that he has risen from the dead. He alone can grant us forgiveness of sins and eternal life. The Gospel message is the only answer to the world's ills and if this offends the leaders of the UN and the world religions as they come together, so be it. This message does not bring harm to anyone, but a better life in this world and the next.

All of these developments tie in exactly with the prophecies of the Bible in the last days. Jesus warned that there would be false messiahs and false prophets who would lead many astray (Matthew 24:5, 11, 24). He said there would be people claiming to be the 'Christ', which is literally happening with New Age gurus making the claim to be the Christ or Messiah for our time.

In Peter's second letter we read,

> *'But there were also false prophets among the people, even as*
> *there will be false teachers among you, who will secretly bring*
> *in destructive heresies, even denying the Lord who bought*
> *them, and bring on themselves swift destruction.'*
>
> (2 Peter 2:1)

Ordained clergy who deny the fundamentals of the Christian
faith are just such false teachers. As a result of their corrupting
influence there will be a great apostasy (departure or
falling away) from the truth, according to Bible prophecies.
This spiritual void will prepare the way for the coming
Antichrist.

Jesus warned that true Christians would be persecuted in
the last days.

> *'But before all these things, they will lay their hands on you*
> *and persecute you, delivering you up to the synagogues and*
> *prisons, and you will be brought before kings and rulers for*
> *My name's sake. But it will turn out for you as an occasion for*
> *testimony. Therefore settle it in your hearts not to meditate*
> *beforehand on what you will answer; for I will give you a*
> *mouth and wisdom which all your adversaries will not be able*
> *to contradict or resist. You will be betrayed even by parents*
> *and brothers, relatives and friends; and they will send some of*
> *you to your death. And you will be hated by all for My name's*
> *sake. But not a hair of your head shall be lost. In your*
> *patience possess your souls.'*   (Luke 21:12–19)

It is not hard to see this becoming a possibility in the
coming days as a result of all the things written about in this
chapter. Already believing Christians face fierce persecution
and martyrdom in many Muslim countries and in China.
The persecutions under Communism in the former Soviet
Union may have eased somewhat for the moment, but there
are new pressures coming particularly from the dominant
religions (Russian Orthodox, Roman Catholic or Islam) in

the countries of the former Soviet bloc. In Russia the Orthodox Church is asserting itself as the legitimate state church and taking measures which are making it more difficult for evangelical Christians to function.

Even in Europe and North America there is a growing challenge to Christianity. Distributing the Bible could become illegal under a proposed European anti-racism law, according to British Law Lord Scott of Foscote. He said this law was meant to normalize member-states' laws against racism: 'The offence in question would almost certainly cover the distribution of Biggles (novels about a fictional World War II pilot). It would probably cover the distribution of the Old Testament as well.'

The Swedish government has changed the constitution in June 2002 to prevent speech or materials opposing homosexuality and any other alternate lifestyles. This means that any Christian declaring homosexuality to be wrong in the sight of God could be breaking the law. Annalie Enochson, a Christian member of Parliament, said, 'That means people coming from the homosexual lobby group could sit in our churches having on the tape recorder and listen to somebody and say, "What you're saying now is against our constitution."' She said anyone convicted of violating the constitutional amendment could spend six months to four years in jail.

The arrival of a movement towards a world government backed by an anti-Christian world religion is a sure sign of the end of this age. The biggest challenge facing this system will be the Middle East. Jerusalem is the point at which the three monotheistic religions, Judaism, Christianity and Islam, meet. It is also the place where religious tension runs highest on the earth. It is no accident that this is the case and in the next three chapters we will look at the Middle East situation in the light of Bible prophecy.

Chapter 6

Israel – Accident of History or Fulfilment of Prophecy?

To answer this question we have to look back over events which happened over a period of nearly 4,000 years, recorded in the Bible. So we will look at this subject as a foundation for the next chapter, which will deal with what is happening in Israel today.

Back in Genesis God made a covenant with Abraham, making him two amazing promises:

> *'Look now toward heaven, and count the stars if you are able to number them ... So shall your descendants be.'*
> (Genesis 15:5)

> *'I am the* Lord, *who brought you out of Ur of the Chaldeans, to give you this land to inherit it.'*   (Genesis 15:7)

Concerning the first promise about having innumerable descendants, Abraham believed that God meant what he said, and so the Lord *'accounted it to him for righteousness'* (i.e. he confirmed the promise on the basis of Abraham's faith). Today a vast number of people claim descent in some form from Abraham.

Concerning the second promise God did something which we find hard to understand, but Abraham would have had no problem understanding. He told Abraham to take some animals, *'a three-year-old heifer, a three-year-old female goat, a three-year-old ram, a turtledove, and a young pigeon'* (Genesis 15:9) and to cut them in two and leave a path between the pieces of the divided animals. Then *'there was a smoking oven and a burning torch that passed between those pieces'* (Genesis 15:17). The smoking oven and burning torch represent the presence of God, which passed between the divided animals.

> *'On the same day the LORD made a covenant with Abram saying, "To your descendants I have given this land, from the river of Egypt to the great river, the River Euphrates."'*
> (Genesis 15:18)

What was all this about? In Abraham's culture if two parties were making a land deal, they did not go to the estate agent and the solicitor. They cut animals in two, passed between the divided animals and said in effect, 'May God (or the gods) do to us as we have done to these animals if we do not keep our word.' Now it was not the best day in the life of those animals when they were cut in two, so the people making the covenant were invoking a curse upon themselves if they did not keep their word. God put Abraham to sleep so that he did not have to pass between the divided animals. By doing this God was communicating something very important. This covenant, by which he was giving the title deeds of ownership of the land to Abraham and his descendants, depended on God's faithfulness not theirs. God would keep his side of the covenant even if Abraham's descendants did not keep theirs.

The major problem from Abraham's point of view was that he did not have even one descendant, let alone a multitude, and his wife Sarah was barren and past childbearing age. So Sarah suggested that Abraham had a child by Hagar, her maid, which he did. So Ishmael was born, but God told

Abraham that this son would not inherit the promise.
Instead Sarah would have a son supernaturally and this child
was to be called Isaac:

> '... Sarah your wife shall bear you a son, and you shall call
> his name Isaac; I will establish My covenant with him for an
> everlasting covenant, and with his descendants after him.
> And as for Ishmael, I have heard you. Behold, I have blessed
> him, and will make him fruitful, and will multiply him
> exceedingly. He shall beget twelve princes, and I will make
> him a great nation.'   (Genesis 17:19–20)

God says that the covenant relating to the land applies to
Isaac and his descendants and not to Ishmael and his
descendants. Ishmael will become a great nation, but the
covenant will be with Isaac. Today the conflict over the land
of Israel involves the Jewish people who claim descent from
Isaac and the Arab people who claim descent from Ishmael.
In Islam, the dominant religion of the Arabs, Abraham
is believed to be a prophet of Islam and the promised son is
believed to be Ishmael and not Isaac. Therefore the promises
given to Abraham go to Ishmael and his descendants, the
Arabs, and not to the Jews.

A few years ago I visited the burial place of Abraham, the
Machpelah in Hebron, and saw a large impressive mosque,
where Muslims were praying with a section separated off for
Jews to pray at, heavily guarded by Israeli soldiers. Is it a
coincidence that one of the major flashpoints of tension in
the conflict today is the site of Abraham's burial place?

The promise given to Abraham was repeated to Isaac
(Genesis 26:2–5) and to Jacob (Genesis 28:13–15). It was
the basis on which God called Moses to lead the Israelites out
of Egypt into the Promised Land (Exodus 6:6–8). As they
made their way through the wilderness God gave them the
Torah (Law/commandments), which he told them to live by.
God also made provision for their failure to keep his
commandments, by giving them a system of sacrifices to be

offered at the Tabernacle and later at the Temple, by means of which their sins could be forgiven.

According to Deuteronomy 28, if they obeyed the Lord they would enjoy the land with good harvests, peace and prosperity, and they would defeat their enemies and be a light to the surrounding nations. But if they worshipped other gods and disobeyed the commandments, a series of disasters would come upon them as a judgement, with the final judgement being removal from the land:

> *'You shall be left few in number, whereas you were as the stars of heaven in multitude, because you would not obey the voice of the* LORD *your God. And it shall be that just as the* LORD *rejoiced over you to do you good and multiply you, so the* LORD *will rejoice over you to destroy you and bring you to nothing; and you shall be plucked from off the land which you go to possess. Then the* LORD *will scatter you among all peoples from one end of the earth to the other.'*
>
> (Deuteronomy 28:62–64)

In these verses we see the reversal of the promise given to Abraham. They would become few in number and be removed from the land. However, even if this most severe judgement took place, they would not be permanently out of the land but would return in God's time.

> *'If any of you are driven out to the farthest parts under heaven, from there the* LORD *your God will gather you, and from there He will bring you. Then the* LORD *your God will bring you to the land which your fathers possessed, and you shall possess it.'* (Deuteronomy 30:4–5)

These verses also say that the return to the land will be accompanied by a return to the Lord, which is actually more important because God is much more interested in where we are spiritually than where we are physically.

Much of the Old Testament can be seen as the outworking of these principles. At times when Israel was faithful to the

Lord they were blessed in the land and overcame their enemies. At the height of Israelite power under David and Solomon they reached for a brief while the promised boundaries of the land (2 Samuel 8:3; 1 Kings 4:21). But more often disobedience to the Lord and the worship of other gods caused Israel to be diminished by the surrounding nations, and eventually to suffer deportation from the land (2 Kings 17:24–5).

Jeremiah was the prophet who God raised up to speak to the generation before the deportation of the Jewish people to Babylon. As a prophet he did three main things:

1. He told them what was going to happen.
2. He gave a reason for it.
3. He gave a promise of restoration.

For forty years Jeremiah warned his generation that the Babylonians were going to invade and destroy Jerusalem and the Temple and take them into captivity unless they repented of their sins. The reason why it was going to happen was the worship of idols and the breaking of God's commandments:

> *'Behold, you trust in lying words that cannot profit. Will you steal, murder, commit adultery, swear falsely, burn incense to Baal, and walk after other gods whom you do not know, and then come and stand before Me in this house which is called by My name and say "We are delivered to do all these abominations"?'*   (Jeremiah 7:8–10)

Far from repenting, the people mocked and rejected Jeremiah, preferring false prophets who said they were going to have peace and safety. But Jeremiah was not just a prophet of doom. He also promised a return from Babylon:

> *'For thus says the LORD: After seventy years are completed at Babylon, I will visit you and perform My good word toward you, and cause you to return to this place. For I know the*

thoughts that I think towards you, says the LORD, *thoughts of peace and not of evil, to give you a future and a hope.'*
(Jeremiah 29:10–11)

This promise was fulfilled when the Persians overthrew the Babylonian Empire and the Persian Emperor Cyrus issued a decree that the Jewish people should return to the Promised Land and rebuild the Temple in Jerusalem (Ezra 1:1–4). In this way the covenant was being fulfilled as the descendants of Abraham returned to the land God promised to Abraham.

Jeremiah also looked beyond the return of the Jewish people to a time when God would make a new covenant with the house of Israel. The terms of this covenant would be different from the covenant God made with Israel when he brought them out of Egypt:

'This is the covenant that I will make with the house of Israel after those days, says the LORD: *I will put My law in their minds, and write it on their hearts; and I will be their God, and they shall be My people. No more shall every man teach his neighbour and every man his brother saying, "Know the* LORD," *for they all shall know Me, from the least of them to the greatest of them says the* LORD. *For I will forgive their iniquity, and their sin I will remember no more.'*
(Jeremiah 31:33–34)

The new covenant points to the Messiah who was to come to deal with the problem of the sin nature, which causes us all to break God's commandments. According to Isaiah 53 this one would be a suffering servant of the Lord:

'He is despised and rejected of men,
A Man of sorrows and acquainted with grief.
And we hid, as it were, our faces from Him:
He was despised, and we did not esteem Him.
Surely He has born our griefs
And carried our sorrows:

> *Yet we esteemed Him stricken,*
> *Smitten by God and afflicted.*
> *But He was wounded for our transgressions,*
> *He was bruised for our iniquities;*
> *The chastisement for our peace was upon Him,*
> *And by His stripes we are healed.*
> *All we like sheep have gone astray;*
> *We have turned, every one to his own way;*
> *And the LORD has laid on Him the iniquity of us all.'*
>
> (Isaiah 53:3–6)

When Jesus came in fulfilment of this and many other prophecies, he brought in the new covenant, through dying as a sacrifice for the sins of the world at the time of the Passover. At the time that the Jewish people were offering the Passover lambs to remember the blood of the lamb, which protected them from the Angel of Death (see Exodus 12), Jesus was put to death by crucifixion in fulfilment of Psalm 22, Daniel 9:26 and Zechariah 12:10. He was the *'lamb of God who takes away the sin of the world'* (John 1:29). He saves all those who come under the protection of his blood from eternal death.

Did the coming of the new covenant mean that God was finished with the Jewish people and that the covenant made with Abraham no longer applied? Much of the Church actually teaches this in so called 'replacement theology' which means that the promises to Israel are now given to the Church. But it is significant that after God gave his promise of the new covenant he said that as long as the sun, the moon and the stars exist, so long will Israel be a nation before the Lord (Jeremiah 31:35–36).

If we look carefully at Jesus' words we discover that in relation to Israel, Jesus too functioned in the same prophetic way that Jeremiah did.

1. He warned of the coming catastrophe.

2. He gave a reason for it.

3. He gave a promise of restoration.

As Jesus was riding into Jerusalem at the beginning of the week which would lead up to his crucifixion and resurrection, he stopped half way down the mount of Olives and wept over the city. He said:

> *'If you had known, even you, especially in this your day, the things that make for your peace! But now they are hidden from your eyes. For the days will come upon you when your enemies will build an embankment around you, surround you and close you in on every side, and level you, and your children within you, to the ground; and they will not leave in you one stone upon another, because you did not know the time of your visitation.'*   (Luke 19:41–44)

Jesus prophesied the coming destruction of Jerusalem and the Temple by the Romans in 70 AD. He told those who believed in him to flee from the city when they saw the armies gathering, because this was going to lead to a time of terrible slaughter and destruction:

> *'For there will be great distress in the land and wrath upon this people. And they shall fall by the edge of the sword, and be led away captive into all nations. And Jerusalem will be trampled by Gentiles until the times of the Gentiles are fulfilled.'*   (Luke 21:23–24)

In these verses Jesus warned of the coming destruction of Jerusalem, and the dispersion of the Jewish people into the lands of the Gentiles. He also gave a reason for it: *'Because you did not know the time of your visitation'*. In other words the dispersion happened because Jesus was not recognised as the Messiah. Of course there were many Jewish people who did recognise Jesus as Messiah and went out into the world to preach the Gospel, but the religious leadership rejected his claim and continued to offer the animal sacrifices for sin in the Temple, after Jesus had come as the final sacrifice for sin. After the sacrifice of Jesus, the offering of the sacrifices became an act of unbelief, rather than faith, because the

blood of the animals had been replaced with the blood of
Jesus as the means whereby sin was atoned for. The Letter to
the Hebrews warns Jewish believers in Jesus not to go back
to the animal sacrifices in the Temple.

For this reason Jesus said,

> *'Your house* [the Temple] *is left to you desolate; for I say to
> you* [i.e. Jerusalem], *you shall see me no more till you say,
> "Blessed is He who comes in the name of the Lord!"'*
>
> (Matthew 23:38–39)

'Blessed is He who comes in the name of the Lord' is not just any
old phrase. In Hebrew it is *'Baruch ha ba be shem adonai'*, the
traditional greeting for the coming Messiah.

In this verse Jesus is pointing to a time when the desolation
of Jerusalem will be reversed and the city will no longer
be *'trampled* [ruled] *by the Gentiles'* (Luke 21:24). What will
cause this change in the fortunes of the city to happen will be
the recognition of Jesus as the Messiah and the resulting
outpouring of the Holy Spirit on those who call on his name.

A number of Old Testament prophecies tie in with this. In
Ezekiel 36–37 there are prophecies of a physical restoration
of Israel, from being a barren land, denuded of its trees and
with its cities forsaken, to becoming a fertile land *'like the
Garden of Eden'*. But more importantly there is also a
prophecy of the spiritual restoration of the people:

> *'For I will take you from among the nations, gather you out of
> all countries, and bring you into your own land. Then I
> will sprinkle clean water on you, and you shall be clean; I will
> cleanse you from all your filthiness and from all your idols.
> I will give you a new heart and put a new spirit within you; I
> will take the heart of stone out of your flesh and give you a
> heart of flesh. I will put My Spirit within you and cause you to
> walk in My statutes, and you will keep My judgements and do
> them. Then you shall dwell in the land that I gave to your
> fathers; you shall be My people and I will be your God.'*
>
> (Ezekiel 36:24–28)

This passage points to Israel being born of the flesh and then born of the Spirit, the very process which Jesus spoke to Nicodemus about when he said:

> *'That which is born of the flesh is flesh, and that which is born of the Spirit is spirit. Do not marvel that I said to you, "You must be born again."'*   (John 3:6–7)

Several scriptures point to the method by which God is going to bring Israel to this point of spiritual rebirth – a time of unique trouble:

> *'For thus says the LORD:*
> *"We have heard a voice of trembling,*
> *Of fear, and not of peace.*
> *Ask now, and see,*
> *Whether a man is ever in labour with child?*
> *So why do I see every man with his hands on his loins*
> *Like a woman in labour,*
> *And all faces turned pale?*
> *Alas! For that day is great,*
> *So that none is like it;*
> *And it is the time of Jacob's trouble,*
> *But he shall be saved out of it."'*   (Jeremiah 30:5–7)

See also Ezekiel 38–39, Daniel 12, Joel 2–3, Zechariah 12–14, Matthew 24, Luke 21 and Revelation 6–19.

This time of trouble involves all nations and precedes the event known in the Old Testament as the Day of the Lord and in the New Testament as the Second Coming of Jesus Christ. But before the final time of trouble begins Israel will sign a 'peace settlement' with the coming world ruler. He is a deceiver, also known as the beast or Antichrist, and the treaty turns out to be a *'covenant with death'* (Isaiah 28:15) leading to Israel being persecuted and brought to the brink of annihilation (Daniel 9:27; 11:29–12:1; Zechariah 12–14; Revelation 12, 16).

In this time of trouble God is seeking to correct something, which Israel has got wrong:

> ' "For I am with you," says the LORD, "to save you;
> Though I make a full end of all nations where I have
>   scattered you,
> Yet I will not make a complete end of you.
> But I will correct you in justice,
> And will not let you go altogether unpunished." '
>
> (Jeremiah 30:11)

What could this be? Israeli treatment of the Palestinians? The fact that Israel is a secular state? All the different branches of Judaism and the often hostile relations between them? Or the identity of the Messiah?

If you were to ask 100 Jewish people how they would identify the Messiah, you would come up with maybe not 100, but certainly a good number of different answers. These are some of the main ones I have heard:

1. Messiah is a great man who will create world peace, rebuild the Temple in Jerusalem and bring the Jewish people back to the Torah.

2. Messiah is Rabbi Schneerson of Lubavitch, who died in 1994 and who will rise again from the dead.

3. There is no personal Messiah, but there will be a Messianic age in which people will live in peace and harmony together and wars will cease.

4. There is no Messiah and the whole idea is a superstition, which Jewish people need to put behind them so they can work out their problems by themselves.

The crisis in the Middle East is creating an interest in the issue of the Messiah amongst Jewish people today. In an article on the Orthodox Jewish website, 'Aish', Rabbi Wilson has written:

We are living in very turbulent times, to say the least. Whereas only two years ago the world and the people of Israel were optimistic about a peaceful solution to the Middle East conflict, today that optimism has been replaced by fear and depression. Fear of unbridled and senseless terrorism, and depression, from what appears to be a no-win situation for the State of Israel.

Now, more than ever before over the last 50 years, the Jewish people, and even the world in general, need a saviour. We need someone who can, somehow, perhaps even mystically, bring about more than just a tenuous ceasefire between two warring peoples. We need some-one who can, once and for all, bring an end to all human conflict, especially in the Middle East. And, if he can do that, a tall order, then perhaps he would also be able to destroy whatever other evil exists in the world. As he engineers this long-dreamed-of world peace, let him make unethical and immoral behaviour a thing of the past, too. In other words, this saviour, if he is truly a saviour, should usher in a permanent utopian society where virtuous living is the main theme and second- (if not first) nature. And, what shall we call this modern-day hero of Biblical proportions? In Judaism, he has always been called 'Moshiach' (Messiah), 'the anointed one', because, as a Jewish king he is to be anointed upon taking office, so-to-speak.

Of course Orthodox Judaism strongly denies that this Messiah is Jesus. In a book called *The Real Messiah* Rabbi Aryeh Kaplan rejects Jesus as Messiah and points to a Messiah figure who does not sound too different from some of the New Age messianic hopes now being propagated. He describes the coming Messiah as 'a charismatic leader greater than any other in man's history. Imagine a political genius surpassing all others. With the vast communication networks now at our disposal, he could spread his message to the entire world and change the very fabric of society'.

He describes a possible scenario, which brings him to power.

> One possible scenario could involve the Middle East situation. This is a problem that involves all the world powers. Now imagine a Jew, a Tzadik (literally a 'righteous one') solving this thorny problem. It would not be inconceivable that such a demonstration of statesmanship and political genius would place him in a position of world leadership. The major powers would listen to such an individual.

He goes on to describe how he would regather the exiles to Israel, cause the Temple to be rebuilt and teach all mankind to live in peace and follow God's teachings. He concludes,

> As society reaches toward perfection and the world becomes increasingly godly, men will begin to explore the transcendental more and more. As the prophet said (Isaiah 11:9), 'For all the earth shall be full of the knowledge of God, as the waters cover the sea.' More and more people will achieve the mystical union of prophecy, as foretold by Joel, 'And it shall come to pass afterward that I will pour out My spirit on all flesh, and your sons and your daughters shall prophesy.'

Jewish messianic hopes centre on a great man coming to make world peace and rescue Israel, but the biblical prophecies show that this is a vain hope and will lead to deep disillusion and betrayal. These prophecies also give a clue to the true identity of the Messiah. The prophet Zechariah has some amazing information on this subject. He describes a world conflict over the status of Jerusalem, a question which will not just affect the countries of the region, but the whole world:

> *'And it shall happen in that day that I will make Jerusalem a very heavy stone for all peoples; all who would heave it away*

> *will surely be cut in pieces, though all nations of the earth are*
> *gathered against it.'* (Zechariah 12:3)

When the armies of the world gather together against Jerusalem to battle, God says,

> *'I will pour on the house of David and on the inhabitants of*
> *Jerusalem the Spirit of grace and supplication; then they will*
> *look on Me whom they have pierced; they will mourn for Him*
> *as one mourns for his only son.'* (Zechariah 12:10)

Following this Zechariah says,

> *'The* L<small>ORD</small> *will go forth*
> *And fight against those nations,*
> *As He fights in the day of battle.*
> *And in that day His feet will stand on the Mount of Olives,*
> *Which faces Jerusalem on the east…*
> *And the* L<small>ORD</small> *shall be King over all the earth.'*
> (Zechariah 14:3–4, 9)

These scriptures fit in exactly with the message of Jesus. He is revealed in the Gospel as the only Son who has been 'pierced', dying by crucifixion, in order to redeem the world, and who will come the second time to judge the world according to how we have responded to his message.

Jesus gave his teaching on his second coming on the Mount of Olives, just outside Jerusalem (Matthew 24; Mark 13; Luke 21), the same place Zechariah says the Lord is coming to in order to save Israel. Jesus ascended into heaven from there and the angel spoke to the disciples saying:

> *'This same Jesus who was taken up from you into heaven, will*
> *so come in like manner as you saw Him go into heaven.'*
> (Acts 1:11)

The event described in Zechariah when Israel looks on one who has been pierced will be the same event as the one I have already quoted in Matthew 23:39 when Jesus said concerning Jerusalem, *'You shall see Me no more until you say, "Blessed is He who comes in the name of the LORD!"'*. When Jesus is welcomed and accepted as Messiah by the Jewish people, he will come to the earth and finally bring peace to Israel, thus fulfilling the prophecy of Isaiah:

> *'Now it shall come to pass in the latter days*
> *That the mountain of the LORD's house*
> *Shall be established on the top of the mountains,*
> *And shall be exalted above the hills;*
> *And all nations shall flow to it.*
> *Many people shall come and say,*
> *"Come, and let us go up to the mountain of the LORD,*
> *To the house of the God of Jacob;*
> *He will teach us His ways,*
> *And we shall walk in His paths."*
> *For out of Zion shall go forth the law,*
> *And the word of the LORD from Jerusalem.*
> *He shall judge between the nations,*
> *And shall rebuke many people;*
> *They shall beat their swords into ploughshares,*
> *And their spears into pruning hooks;*
> *Nation shall not lift up sword against nation,*
> *Neither shall they learn war anymore.'*   (Isaiah 2:2–4)

Chapter 7

The Battle for Israel

From the Bible passages quoted in the last chapter we should expect to see the following sequence of events taking place regarding Israel.

1. The Jewish people scattered from the land of Israel and dwelling amongst the Gentile nations of the earth.
2. The Jewish people keeping their identity in the lands of dispersion and regathering to Israel.
3. This regathering to be in unbelief.
4. A time of trouble taking place during which the nations of the world gather against Israel.
5. A false peace plan.
6. Out of this time of trouble a spiritual rebirth to take place, as a result of which the remnant of Israel calls on the name of Yeshua (Jesus) for salvation.
7. The physical return of Jesus the Messiah to the earth to rule and reign from Jerusalem during the Millennium (Messianic Age).

When we look at Jewish history and current events in Israel what do we see? The Jewish people have been scattered to the nations of the world, where for the most part they have been treated shamefully, especially by those who claimed to be Christians. Many have been persecuted as the 'Christ killers' when Jesus himself said, *'I lay down my life, that I may take it again. No one takes it from me, but I lay it down of myself'* (John 10:17–18). Whether it was in Islamic lands or in Christendom they kept their identity and never lost their desire to go back to the land of Israel. Each year at Passover they ended the meal with the words *'L'shana ha ba b'irushalayim'* ('Next Year in Jerusalem'). In Russia and Poland, at one time the home of the majority of Jews, they would remember the New Year of Trees in January. There is not much chance of planting trees in the snowy lands of the north in January, but they were remembering the time when trees were planted in the Holy Land. By such reminders the desire to return to the land of Israel was kept alive through the long years of exile.

According to Ezekiel 36 during the time of this exile the land would become *'desolate wastes'* with *'cities that are forsaken'* (Ezekiel 36:4). This was exactly the condition Mark Twain, the American author of *Tom Sawyer* and *Huckleberry Finn*, found when he visited Palestine, at that time a backwater of the Turkish Ottoman Empire, in 1867. He described it in his book, *The Innocents Abroad*:

> Of all the lands there are for dismal scenery, I think Palestine must be the prince ... It is a hopeless, dreary, heart broken land ... Palestine sits in sackcloth and ashes. Over it broods the spell of a curse that has withered its fields and fettered its energies ... Palestine is desolate and unlovely.

Of Jerusalem he wrote:

> Rags, wretchedness, poverty and dirt abound, lepers, cripples, the blind and the idiotic assail you on every hand. Jerusalem is mournful, dreary and lifeless. I would not desire to live here.

By the late 19th century Zionist pioneers, mainly from Russia and Ukraine, began to immigrate into Palestine and to purchase land from absentee Arab landlords. They drained the swamps and planted trees and began the process of turning the barren land into a fertile place. The population of Jerusalem swelled from about 15,000 in 1865 to 45,472 in 1896, of whom 28,112 were Jews. The prophecy of the physical rebirth of Israel was beginning:

> *'But you, O mountains of Israel, you shall shoot forth your branches and yield your fruit to My people Israel, for they are about to come. For I am indeed for you and I will turn to you, and you shall be tilled and sown. I will multiply men upon you, all the house of Israel, all of it; and the cities shall be inhabited and the ruins rebuilt.'* (Ezekiel 36:8–10)

At around this time the Zionist movement began to organise seriously. At the first Zionist Congress in Basel, Switzerland, Zionist leader, Theodor Herzl, wrote in his diary on 29th August 1897:

At Basel I founded the Jewish State. If I were to say this today, I would be greeted with universal laughter. In five years, perhaps, and certainly in fifty, everyone will see it.

On 29th November 1947, exactly 50 years later, the General Assembly of the United Nations passed by 33 votes to 13, with 10 abstentions (including the British), the resolution to partition Palestine, which led to the creation of the State of Israel in May 1948.

Herzl dreamed of an orderly return to Zion from the nations of the world. In fact the return and the establishment of the State of Israel in 1948 came through the agony of the Holocaust and the destruction of one-third of the world's Jewish population. It also came in the teeth of fierce opposition from the Arab world and from the British government, which had the Mandate for Palestine at that time. Despite all this, the United Nations took the decision to partition Palestine and allow the establishment of a tiny Jewish state on a fraction of the land originally promised by the British government through the Balfour Declaration.

The immediate and continuing response of the surrounding Arab nations was to seek to eliminate the Jewish state. At times Arab leaders like Nasser of Egypt almost literally quoted the words of Psalm 83:4,

> '*Come, and let us cut them off from being a nation,*
> *That the name of Israel may be remembered no more.*'

In verses 6–8 of this Psalm there is a list of nations, which can be identified as Jordan, Egypt, Lebanon, Gaza, Syria and Iraq. In 1948, 1967 and 1973 Israel has had to fight wars for survival against numerically superior armies from these countries bent on pushing the Jewish state into the sea.

In 1964 the Palestine Liberation Organisation (PLO) was set up with the intention of 'liberating' Israeli lands and returning them to Arab control. This was before the Six-Day War so the land intended for 'liberation' was the territory of Israel as established in 1948, not the area of the West Bank and Gaza, which is today being claimed for a Palestinian State. The Palestine National Covenant, the Charter of the PLO, calls for the 'liberation of Palestine' from the 'Zionist invasion' by 'armed struggle' and 'aims at the elimination of Zionism in Palestine' (i.e. the destruction of Israel). It denies that the Jews are a nation or that they have 'historical or religious ties with Palestine'. It states that only 'the Jews who normally resided in Palestine until the beginning of the Zionist invasion will be considered Palestinians'.

Therefore it denies Israel's right to exist in any form and commits the organisation to a programme aiming at the replacement of Israel with a Palestinian State from which the majority of Jewish citizens would be expelled. Article 33 of the Covenant states that: 'This Charter shall not be amended save by a vote of a majority of two thirds of the total membership of the National Congress of the PLO taken at a special session convened for that purpose.' Despite claims to the contrary such a meeting has never taken place and therefore the Charter remains the guiding principle of the PLO. In pursuing these aims the PLO became the first organisation to use the tactics of modern terrorism, which have been copied by other terrorist organisations throughout the world.

In spite of all that has been thrown against her, Israel has survived and through victories won in 1948 and 1967 ended up with control of more territory than was originally allotted to her by the UN. The Six-Day War in 1967 brought the whole of the West Bank (Judea and Samaria), the Golan Heights, the Gaza Strip and the Sinai Peninsula under Israeli control. In August 1967 Israel offered to return these territories in return for peace and recognition by the Arab world, but the response of the Arab nations at the Khartoum Conference was: 'No recognition, no peace, no negotiations with Israel.' Israel did return the Sinai to Egypt after Israeli Prime Minister, Menachem Begin, and Egyptian President, Anwar Sadat, signed the Camp David Agreement in 1978.

For Jewish people the capture of the West Bank meant the regaining of the most significant places in their history from a biblical point of view, including Hebron, Nablus (Shechem), Bethlehem, Jericho and of course the Old City of Jerusalem. From 1948 to 1967 Jerusalem had been a city divided by a wall with barbed wire and checkpoints as Berlin was during the days of the Cold War. The new part of the city, where the Knesset (Israeli parliament) is housed, was under Israeli control. The historic Old City was under Jordanian control. Here were the holy places, sacred to Jews, Christians and Muslims – the Church of the Holy Sepulchre, the Via Dolorosa, the Dome of the Rock and Al Aqsa mosques (the Temple Mount), and the Jewish Quarter with the Western (Wailing) Wall. During the entire period of Jordanian rule all Jews were expelled from the Old City and unable to pray at the Western Wall.

When the Israelis entered the Old City of Jerusalem on 7th June 1967, the Chief of Staff of the Israeli Defence Force, Moshe Dayan, stood at the Western Wall and said, 'We have regained our holiest place, never again to depart.' Israel adopted an open policy to all the holy places for all faiths. At the same time the Jewish Quarter was resettled with *'yeshivoth'* (study centres) being established for Orthodox Jews and attracting students from all over the world. The focus of worship of Jewish people worldwide became the Western Wall.

However the most holy place for Jewish people, the Temple Mount, remained under Islamic control. In the rest of the West Bank and in parts of Gaza, Jewish settlements were established, especially in areas of religious significance like Hebron. These settlements have become a major source of conflict between Israel and the Palestinians.

As a result of this the stage was set for the end time conflict described in the Bible. Jerusalem became the *'burdensome stone'* of Zechariah 12:3, the irresolvable point of conflict, which involved not just Israel and the Arab world, but *'all nations'*. For the Arab world any solution, which left the Old City of Jerusalem in Jewish hands, was not acceptable. For the Jewish world Jerusalem became the indivisible capital of Israel and could not be handed back to the Arabs.

By virtue of its religious significance to Jews, Christians and Muslims, Jerusalem became the focal point of world attention for millions of people. But this is not the only reason for world attention on this place. The vast oil reserves in the Middle East and the dependence of all nations on the free flow of oil also means that any war over Israel now affects all people whatever their faith or lack of it. Added to this Jerusalem and the whole of Israel are among the most open places on earth for media to operate in, so that any flare up of violence here is inevitably flashed across TV screens around the world. At the time when Zechariah wrote his prophecy the idea that a conflict over Jerusalem could be a subject of concern to the whole world would have seemed ridiculous. In our time it is a reality.

The Six-Day War also increased the outrage and radicalisation of the Islamic world. In Islamic thinking the world is divided into the *'Dar al Islam'* (abode of Islam, meaning territories governed by Muslims) and the *'Dar al Harb'* (abode of war, meaning those lands not under Muslim control). The *'Dar al Harb'* is the object of *'Jihad'* until the Day of

Judgment, with the aim being to bring it under Muslim control. *Jihad* can mean a religious struggle to convert the population to Islam by argument or 'holy war' using force to impose it. Of particular concern is any land which has once been Muslim and for some reason ceases to be controlled by Muslims.

For this reason Israel and the Zionist movement have been the object of *Jihad* in the aggressive sense from the very beginning. For Islam a Jewish state has no place in the Middle East, being situated on territory conquered by the Muslims in 638 AD, and containing sites holy to the Muslims, in particular the Dome of the Rock and Al Aqsa Mosques in Jerusalem. According to Islamic thinking losing this territory to non-Muslims was an insult to Allah, and so the Muslims must regain it. Any Jewish claims to the land based on the covenants of the Bible are discounted because the Muslims believe that the Jews and Christians 'changed the books' (i.e. our Bible is not the original message given by God). The only solution from a strict Muslim point of view is the elimination of Israel and its replacement with a Palestinian Arab state ruled by Muslims. In this state Arab Christians and a small remnant of the Jewish community would be permitted to live as *'Dhimmis'* (people subject to the Muslims).

For the Muslim world the Israeli victory in 1967 was not just a military defeat, but also a reversal of the march of history and a stain on Islam, which must be avenged. In October 1968 the issue of Israel's victory in the Six-Day War was discussed at a conference of The Islamic Research Academy at al-Azhar University in Cairo, the main intellectual centre of the Islamic world. The Grand Imam of the University said, 'It is inconceivable that Allah would grant to the Unbelievers [i.e. the Jews] a way to triumph over the Believers [i.e. the Muslims].' The general conclusion was that these events 'contradicted the design of Allah and the march of history' and that this defeat was a kind of judgement of Allah on the Muslim world because they had been taking on board influences from Western Capitalism and from Soviet

Communism. The answer was to return to pure Islam and so defeat Israel.

This view contributed to the radicalisation of the Islamic world, the overthrow of the Shah in Iran in 1979 in Khomeini's Islamic Revolution, and the rise of fundamentalist Muslim groups, like Hamas and Al Qaeda, which are willing to use terror and extreme violence to gain their ends. Suicide terrorism has been used with devastating effect in the events of 11th September 2001 in America and in terrorist attacks in Israel. Muslim preachers in the Palestinian areas, in Saudi Arabia and throughout the Islamic world regularly issue blood-curdling threats against Israel and the Jewish people.

They often justify these threats with verses from the Koran which encourage such attitudes:

> Fight those who do not believe in Allah, nor in the latter day, nor do they prohibit what Allah and His Apostle have prohibited, nor follow the religion of truth, out of those who have been given the Book, until they pay the tax in acknowledgment of superiority and they are in a state of subjection.   (Sura [chapter] 9 verse 29)

> O you who believe! Do not take the Jews and the Christians for friends; they are friends of each other; and whoever amongst you takes them for a friend, then surely he is one of them; surely Allah does not guide the unjust people.   (Sura 5:51)

Although not explicitly mentioned in the Koran, there is a Hadith, which gives a detailed series of events connected with the end of days. (A Hadith is a saying or tradition, not part of the Koran but given importance in Islamic thinking.) It speaks of Jesus (who is considered to be a prophet in Islam) going to Jerusalem with a lance in his hand with which he will kill a false Messiah. Then he will kill the pigs, break the crosses, demolish churches and kill Christians except those who accept him in the Muslim sense as a prophet and not the

Son of God. Then he will remain on the earth for as long as Allah wills – perhaps for 40 years. Then he will die and the Muslims will pray over him and bury him.

Many Muslim preachers are speaking today of an apocalyptic scenario involving a great war with the Jewish people over Jerusalem. This will be the first stage of the planned Islamic conquest of the whole world. They are confident of victory and see no need for any compromise with Israel or the West. The following is an extract from a sermon given by Imam Sheikh Ibrahim Madhi in Gaza on 12th April 2002 and broadcast live on Palestinian TV. It is typical of the kind of incitement being given today in mosques throughout the Islamic world.

We are convinced of the future victory of Allah; we believe that one of these days, we will enter Jerusalem as conquerors, enter Jaffa as conquerors, enter Haifa as conquerors, and all of Palestine as conquerors, as Allah has decreed. [By referring to Haifa and Jaffa, Israeli coastal cities, he means that the Muslims will eliminate Israel.] Anyone who does not attain martyrdom in these days should wake in the middle of the night and say: 'My God, why have you deprived me of martyrdom for your sake? For the martyr lives next to Allah.'

The Jews await the false Jewish messiah, while we await, with Allah's help, the Mahdi and Jesus, peace be upon him. Jesus' pure hands will murder the false Jewish messiah. Where? In the city of Lod, in Palestine. Palestine will be, as it was in the past, a graveyard for the invaders. A reliable Hadith [tradition] says: 'The Jews will fight you, but you will be set to rule over them.' What could be more beautiful than this tradition? 'The Jews will fight you' – that is, the Jews have begun to fight us. 'You will be set to rule over them' – Who will set the Muslim to rule over the Jew? Allah. When the Jew hides behind the rock and the tree, the rock and tree will say: 'Oh Muslim, oh servant of Allah, a Jew hides behind me, come and kill him.'

We believe in this Hadith. We are convinced also that this Hadith heralds the spread of Islam and its rule over all the land. Oh beloved, look to the East of the earth, find Japan and the ocean; look to the West of the earth, find some country and the ocean. Be assured that these will be owned by the Muslim nation, as the Hadith says, 'from the ocean to the ocean'.

Similar sermons are being preached all over the Middle East, stirring up a spirit of hatred which will bring the Muslim nations into all out war aimed at Israel's destruction as described in Psalm 83 quoted above. In this Psalm there is a reference to Zeba and Zalmunna, who said, *'Let us take for ourselves the pastures of God for a possession'* (v. 12). We find reference to Zeba and Zalmunna in Judges 8. They were kings of Midian, leaders of the army, which came against Israel in the days of Gideon. In Judges 8:21 we read:

'Gideon arose and killed Zeba and Zalmunna, and took the crescent ornaments that were on their camels' necks.'

The Hebrew word used for 'ornaments' is *'ha saharonim'*, an unusual word, which is correctly translated in the New King James Version as 'crescent ornaments'. The crescent ornament showed dedication to the moon god of paganism.

Today there is a world religion, which also uses the crescent as its symbol – Islam. Islam embodies everything spoken of in this Psalm in its attitude towards Israel. It is the dominant religion of the countries which surround Israel. Those countries have made an alliance against Israel, aiming at the elimination of the Jewish state. While they propose a treaty which offers 'peace', which we will look at in the next chapter, their real aim is the destruction of Israel.

They wish to take possession of the land of Israel, which is considered to be part of the *Dar al Islam* (house of Islam). The Bible says Israel is the land which God gave to Abraham in a covenant, which he confirmed with Isaac and Jacob (Genesis 15; 26:2–5; 28:3–4). Islam has changed the message to make

Ishmael not Isaac the inheritor of the covenant, which contradicts the Bible (Genesis 17:19–21). Therefore in their view Muslims, as descendants of Abraham and Ishmael, should rule over Jews, the descendants of Abraham, Isaac and Jacob. For this reason it does not matter how many concessions Israel makes, Islamic militants will not make a real peace with Israel. Their hostility has nothing to do with the way Israel treats the Palestinians. It is based on the fact that Israel exists.

This fact was made clear after the bombing of the Hebrew University in Jerusalem on 1st August 2002 by Hamas terrorists, when seven people were killed and 90 wounded. Claiming responsibility for the attack Hamas spokesman Abdel Rantisi said terrorist attacks will continue until all Jews leave Israel.

When Israel responds to such attacks and civilians are killed, along with the terrorists responsible, the world comes down upon them with heavy condemnation. Today Israel has become the whipping boy of the world's media, blamed for taking defensive measures against terrorists who are open in their aim to wipe out the Jewish state. Most Israelis would like to reach a peace settlement with the Arabs. But they do not want to be thrown into the sea. Israel's growing unpopularity in the world also ties in with Bible prophecies, which indicate that Israel will be alone in the last days, and only God's intervention will save her.

Chapter 8

Peace, Peace

There is another side to Islam and to the whole situation, which appears to be running in the opposite direction to what I have written in the previous chapter. In an interview for *Newsweek* (3rd December 2001), Tony Blair said, 'True Islam is immensely tolerant and open.' Many western leaders promote the idea that there is a moderate form of Islam, which wants to make peace with Israel and the western world.

On this basis Israeli Prime Minister Rabin and PLO Chairman Arafat signed the Oslo Accords in September 1993, announcing, 'It is time to put an end to decades of confrontation and conflict and to strive to live in peaceful coexistence and mutual dignity and security.' The hope was that an Israeli withdrawal from territories captured by Israel in the Six-Day War and an Arab renunciation of violence against Israel and recognition of the Jewish state would make way for a comprehensive Middle East peace plan.

At the time I wrote in *Light for the Last Days* (October 1993) that the agreement would break down over Jerusalem. Even as it was being signed the leaders were making mutually exclusive claims on the city. Rabin said, 'Jerusalem remains under Israeli sovereignty and our capital.' But Arafat said, 'Whoever would relinquish an inch of Jerusalem is not an Arab or a Muslim.'

Seven years later the Oslo Agreement did break down primarily over the issue of Jerusalem. In July 2000, at talks for a final peace deal in the USA, Israeli Prime Minister Barak offered Arafat far more than anyone, including US President Clinton, expected. There was agreement on most of the territorial issues. The sticking point was Jerusalem. Barak offered Arafat half of the Old City of Jerusalem and control of the Arab neighbourhoods both in the city and surrounding it (something Rabin had refused to offer in 1993). He agreed that the Palestinian State would have authority over the Temple Mount, that they could fly their flag there and that Arafat could have his office on the Temple Mount. He even spoke of two capitals, one called Jerusalem as capital of Israel and the other called Al Quds as capital of Palestine.

Arafat rejected this offer to the dismay of Clinton, refusing to compromise over the Palestinian demand for sovereignty over the whole of the Old City of Jerusalem. As this includes the Jewish Quarter and Jewish holy places, there was no way Barak could accept this demand, without provoking total rejection from the Israeli population, so bringing down his government. At the meeting of the Islamic Conference Organisation in Morocco a month later in August, Arafat declared, 'Our struggle will continue and we won't concede even an inch of the city.' Jerusalem remained the *'burdensome stone'* just as Zechariah prophesied 2,500 years ago.

Out of that rejection came the bloody uprising, which has claimed thousands of lives and brought misery and fear to both sides. The threat of the situation spiralling out of control and sparking a general war in the Middle East has focused the minds of politicians all around the world. 'It is clear that American mediation efforts have failed and we need new mediation before the Israel-Palestinian conflict balloons into an all out regional war,' said European Commission President Romano Prodi.

In March 2002 Saudi Prince Abdullah launched a new initiative calling for 'full normalisation of relations with Israel' in exchange for 'withdrawal from all the occupied territory in accordance with UN resolutions, including in Jerusalem.' This proposal demanded much greater concessions from Israel than were previously put forward in the Oslo Accords, but it has now become the main proposal on the table. If accepted it would mean Israel withdrawing from all of the West Bank and Gaza, the Golan Heights and the whole of the Old City of Jerusalem. It would leave Israel perilously exposed with Syria regaining the Golan Heights in the north and coming right down to the northern shore of the Lake of Galilee and with the Palestinians in control of areas vital to Israel's defence along the Jordan Valley and the heights of Judea and Samaria.

In return Israel would have a peace treaty with the Arab nations. How much would this peace treaty be worth? From past experience not much. When Yasser Arafat shook hands with Yitzhak Rabin on the White House lawn in September 1993 he pledged to seek a peaceful solution to the conflict and renounce terrorism. Since that time he has done nothing of the kind.

A reason for this is to be found in the strategy, which was agreed on by the PLO in 1974. Known as the '10 Points Phased Doctrine' this strategy aimed to set up a mini-state as the first step in 'liberating Palestine'. The statement of the Palestine National Council said, amongst other things:

> Once it is established, the Palestinian national authority will strive to achieve a union of the confrontation countries, with the aim of completing the liberation of all Palestinian territory and as a step along the road to comprehensive Arab unity.

In other words this state would be a springboard for the final goal, which is the elimination of Israel.

When Arafat was criticised by some of his own side for making a treaty with Israel he replied that this was the phased policy which had already been agreed on. He also referred on several occasions to the Truce of Hudaybiyya, which Mohammed made with the residents of Mecca at the beginning of his conquest of Arabia. In this treaty Mohammed made peace with the people of Mecca (who rejected his claim to be a prophet) and withdrew his forces to Medina. At the time of making the peace treaty the Meccans were stronger than Mohammed's forces. Within two years Mohammed's forces were stronger than the Meccans, so he abandoned the peace treaty and made war, defeating the opposition to Islam in Mecca and imposing it by force.

This made a precedent for Islam in which you can make an armistice with an enemy while he is stronger than you and if the armistice is good for the Islamic community. But when your enemy is perceived to be weaker, war is imperative and is demanded by the Koran. You are no longer bound by the peace treaty you made previously.

It is interesting that in 1995 the Mufti of Saudi Arabia, Sheikh Abdel Aziz Bin-Baz, handed down a religious ruling to the effect that Islamic law does not rule out peace with Israel. However, he went on to explain that 'peace with Israel is permissible only on condition that it is a temporary peace, until the Moslems build up the military strength needed to expel the Jews.' By this logic the 'peace plan' is merely a trick to weaken Israel in order to deliver the final blow when the Islamic forces are strong enough.

In Psalm 83 we read that the countries which are seeking the destruction of Israel *'have consulted together with one consent. They form a confederacy against you'*. In other words they have a hidden agenda. They may say words of peace to those who want to hear that message (primarily the leaders of the USA and EU) but their real aim is the opposite one. This was spelled out clearly by Abu Jihad, Arafat's deputy, at the PLO's Algiers summit in 1988:

What we are doing is carrying out a two-phase strategy. This is a policy that says first we get a Palestinian State next to Israel, then we use it as a base to destroy what remains of Israel. In order to get to the first step we must persuade the world of our bona fides, that we don't intend to carry out the second phase.

The last sentence here clearly points to a deception aimed at the rest of the world. The impression must be given that the establishment of a Palestinian State will mean the end of the conflict and that the PLO has abandoned its aim of eliminating Israel. In fact it will mean that the next stage of eliminating Israel will be much easier to achieve, with the consent of the world community.

In the book of Isaiah 28:14–22 we find a very interesting passage, which we will look at in more detail in the next chapter. This passage speaks of Israel making an agreement, which they hope will protect them from invasion, but will turn out to be a *'covenant with death'* based on lies and deception. This ties in very much with the present scenario in which a peace plan is being proposed.

Apart from the Islamic dimension there is also a link in this process to Rome. The key scripture making this connection is Daniel 9:26–27. In view of the difficulty of this passage I have put the interpretation in brackets:

> *'And after the sixty-two weeks*
> *Messiah shall be cut off, but not for Himself*
>   [the death of Jesus on the cross];
> *And the people of the prince who is to come*
> *Shall destroy the city and the sanctuary*
>   [the destruction of Jerusalem and its
>   Temple in 70 AD by the Romans,
>   40 years after the crucifixion and
>   resurrection of Jesus].
> *The end of it shall be with a flood,*
> *And till the end of the war desolations are determined*
>   [following the first coming of Messiah there
>   will be a prolonged period of wars and the
>   desolation of Jerusalem].
> *Then he* [the prince who is to come] *shall confirm a*
>   *covenant* [peace agreement] *with many for one week*
>   [7 years – see Genesis 29:27];
> *But in the middle of the week*
> *He shall bring an end to sacrifice and offering.*

> *And on the wing of abominations shall be one who makes
>   desolate*
> *Even until the consummation which is determined,*
> *Is poured out on the desolate.'*

In Daniel's prophecy *'the prince to come'* is the Beast or Antichrist described in Revelation. According to this passage the people from whom the Antichrist will come have destroyed Jerusalem and the Temple at some time previous to his arrival. The people who destroyed the Temple were the Romans, so *'the prince to come'* will also have a connection to Rome. He will offer a peace covenant to Israel, but will turn out to be a deceiver who will break his word and instead bring desolation until he meets his appointed end at the return of the Messiah.

This links up with the information given in Chapters 4 and 5 of this book and brings Europe into the region. Europe's desire to exert its influence in the world has extended to the Middle East region, where it is seeking to mediate a peace settlement between Israel and the Palestinians. The Arab world prefers European mediation to American because they consider America to be too sympathetic to Israel and Europe to be more sympathetic to their viewpoint. Given Europe's long history of anti-Semitism and bias against Israel this is not good news for Israel.

It is interesting also that both Israel and the Palestinians have made representations to Rome and the Vatican. The papacy has a vital interest in the 'holy places' in Jerusalem and as we saw in Chapter 5 is very concerned for promoting a peace movement that will involve all religions as well as governments. For obvious reasons there is nowhere on earth where such a movement is more relevant than Jerusalem and the 'Holy Land'.

When the Pope visited Damascus in May 2001 he said,

> We know that real peace can only be achieved if there is a new attitude of understanding and respect between the three Abrahamic religions, Christianity, Islam and

Judaism ... There is a need for a new spirit of dialogue and cooperation between Christians and Muslims. Together we must proclaim to the world that the name of God is a name of peace and a summons to peace.

The Pope's efforts to reconcile Roman Catholicism and Islam in 2001 complemented his visit to Jerusalem in 2000 when he called for reconciliation with Judaism.

There have been a number of moves to increase the involvement of the Vatican and the European Union in the peace process. The end of the standoff at Bethlehem's Church of the Nativity in May 2002 was achieved after negotiations between Israeli foreign minister, Shimon Peres, and Italian Prime Minister, Silvio Berlusconi and top Vatican officials.

This is not the first time Shimon Peres has been involved in discussions with the Vatican relating to the Middle East peace process. On 10th September 1993, just three days before signing the Oslo Accords in Washington, the Italian newspaper, *La Stampa*, reported that Peres, who was then Israeli Foreign Minister, had concluded a secret deal with the Vatican to hand over sovereignty of Jerusalem's Old City to the Vatican. In May 1994, Marek Halter, a French intellectual and friend of Peres, told the Israeli weekly magazine *Hashishi* that he had personally delivered a letter from Peres to the Pope in September 1993 in which he promised to internationalise Jerusalem, granting UN political control of the Old City and the Vatican control of the holy sites there. The UN would grant the PLO a capital within its new territory.

Although it is hard to verify this story, it has been circulating in Israel for a number of years and points to the fact that a great deal of secret diplomacy has been going on behind the scenes involving big players in world government and world religious circles. It is possible that Peres is an insider in the 'New World Order' working on behalf of the globalist programme within the Israeli government. It is certain that the EU has been sending funds to the peace camp in Israel in order to promote the kind of deal over Jerusalem mentioned above.

The Vatican has a clear interest in keeping a controlling influence in the Old City of Jerusalem and the holy sites there. While not supportive of Israel's claim on the city, the last thing they want is a radical Islamic regime to take control in place of Israel as this could shut them out of these most important shrines of Christendom. Therefore the proposal has been made that the city should be internationalised. The view of the EU and the USA is the same. The only solution would seem to be some kind of international peacekeeping force, which has been proposed by many interested parties (but is currently strongly resisted by the Israelis).

European Union leaders have declared they stand 'ready to contribute fully to peace-building' and support an international peace conference, jointly hosted by the EU, the US, the UN, and Russia, to discuss with the Israelis and the Palestinians security, political and economic issues in the Middle East. Both Prime Minister Sharon and Shimon Peres have expressed interest in Rome being the venue. Sharon said: 'We have excellent relations with Rome and my personal relations with Prime Minister Berlusconi are great.'

Berlusconi also has good relations with the Palestinians, as Italy has proposed a 'Marshall Plan' to help revive the Palestinian economy. Rome mayor Walter Veltroni offered the Eternal City as a possible location for the talks, saying, 'If a peace conference for the Middle East is held, then Rome would be the ideal venue.'

From the point of view of biblical prophecy it is highly likely that some kind of peace deal will emerge involving Rome and the European Union acting as mediators. Whether that involves the characters in power at the time of writing remains to be seen, but in many ways we see the stage being set for a peace treaty, which will tie in with the prophecies of the Bible.

It is interesting that the Oslo Accords broke down exactly seven years after the signing ceremony in Washington. Instead of a final peace ceremony, the world's TV screens were filled with images of Israeli soldiers fighting with

Palestinians on the Temple Mount, as the Al Aqsa Intifada began. Oslo was a kind of dry run of the final peace treaty, which is coming, which will end up seven years later with the armies of the world gathering at Armageddon!

Chapter 9

The Rider on the White Horse

So far in this book we have looked at current developments taking place in the world. In all these developments there are two common themes:

1. They tie in with the prophecies of the Bible for the last days of this age.
2. They are pushing the world in the direction of a globalist or 'one world' solution for our present troubles.

According to the Bible, although there have been times of trouble all through history, there will be a unique time of trouble in the days immediately before the second coming of Christ to the earth, known as the Great Tribulation. This is a seven-year period divided in two so that the final $3\frac{1}{2}$ years are the most intense time of trouble the world has ever known. At this time the world will come under the control of a man known as the Antichrist or Beast who will be Satan's man on earth. He will have a sidekick called the False Prophet who will direct people to worship the Antichrist as a god. The major portion of the Bible which deals with this period is the Book of Revelation, chapters 6 to 19. These chapters are an expansion of Jesus' teaching on the events preceding his second coming to be found in Matthew 24, Mark 13 and Luke 21.

We do not yet see the central characters of this prophecy, the Antichrist and the False Prophet, in their positions of power. If we did there would be little point in even attempting to produce a book like this! However, at the moment the world is on a knife-edge with all kinds of calamities threatening. At some stage in the future something will happen to tip us over the edge and unleash the events of the Great Tribulation on the earth. When this happens the Antichrist will ride onto the world stage and take up his position of power, promising peace and safety, but in fact bringing the final catastrophe of this age. The following are possible scenarios to bring about the rise of the Antichrist:

1.   A limited Middle East war.

2.   A worldwide financial crash.

3.   A terrorist assault using weapons of mass destruction.

4.   A major environmental disaster.

5.   The Rapture of the Church.

6.   A combination of two or more of these things.

Up to this point I have not mentioned number 5 in the above list, so I had better explain what the Rapture of the Church means. This is a teaching, which is controversial, and I can be sure that whatever I write about it, I will receive a pile of letters from people wanting to put me right!

The word 'rapture' is taken from a Latin word meaning to 'catch up' or 'seize away'. (For further information on this subject see Appendix 1.) The Latin word is taken from the Greek word *'harpazo'* which is used in the following verses from 1 Thessalonians 4:16–17, the main basis for the teaching on the Rapture of the Church:

> *'For the Lord Himself will descend from heaven with a shout, with the voice of an archangel, and with the trumpet of God. And the dead in Christ will rise first. Then we who are alive and remain shall be **caught up** to meet the Lord in the air. And thus we shall always be with the Lord.'*

In this passage the Lord comes **for** the saints (i.e. the true believers in Jesus) and meets them **in the air**. In other passages in Scripture (Zechariah 14:5; Jude 14–15 and Revelation 19:14) the Lord comes **with** the saints **to the earth** for his millennial (1,000 year) reign (more on that later!).

The sudden disappearance of millions of people on the earth would certainly create a huge panic on the earth and leave those left behind with some big questions to answer. Jesus described such an event and used it as a warning to people to be ready for his coming at any time:

> *'But as the days of Noah were, so also will the coming of the Son of Man be. For as in the days before the flood, they were eating and drinking, marrying and giving in marriage, until the day that Noah entered the ark, and did not know until the flood came and took them all away, so also will the coming of the Son of Man be. Then two men will be in the field: one will be taken and the other left. Two women will be grinding at the mill: one will be taken and the other left. Watch therefore, for you do not know what hour your Lord is coming. But know this, that if the master of the house had known what hour the thief would come, he would have watched and not allowed his house to be broken into. Therefore you also be ready, for the Son of Man is coming at an hour you do not expect Him.'*
>
> (Matthew 24:37–44)

This passage describes a separation which will take place between those who are taken to be with Jesus and those who are left behind. Whether they are male or female, or outside (in the field) or inside (at the mill), will make no difference. One will be taken and one will be left.

There is a parallel passage in Luke's Gospel, which adds the detail: *'there will be two men in one bed: the one will be taken and the other will be left'* (Luke 17:34). This has nothing to do with homosexuality. What it means is that whether they are awake or asleep will make no difference. One will be taken and one will be left. It is interesting that at any moment in the earth's history on one side of the world it is day where most people will be awake, while on the other side it is night, where most people will be asleep, something the Gospel writers themselves would not have known at the time.

This event will happen unexpectedly as people are going about their normal business, eating, drinking, buying, selling, planting crops, building, getting married. Suddenly one will disappear and one will be left behind. Who will disappear? The true believer in Jesus. Who will be left behind? The unbeliever.

The big question is whether this event happens before or after the Great Tribulation period. If it happens before it means that the second coming is in two stages with Jesus coming first for the believing Church and then seven years later to the earth. If it is after it means that the believers are taken up and return to the earth more or less simultaneously. It also means that most will not survive until this time, being martyred during the Great Tribulation period.

There are those who say that the teaching that the Rapture happens before the Tribulation is a novel doctrine, which the early Church knew nothing of, and is a kind of cop out for weak western Christians who do not want to have their heads chopped off! I believe in the pre-tribulation Rapture and have put some reasons for this in Appendix 1 at the end of this book. However, I do not wish to quarrel with anyone who holds the post-tribulation view and would encourage everyone reading this book to be ready to meet the Lord at any time and also to be ready to suffer for the faith, even to the point of martyrdom, if called upon so to do.

Whichever view of the timing of the Rapture is correct, the prospect of a conflict taking place in the Middle East with a major economic shake up as a result, would cause people all over the world to be in a state of extreme fear and insecurity. No doubt many would be looking for answers. The book of Revelation indicates that when the time of trouble begins people will divide into two radically different camps.

In chapter 7 we read of a great harvest of people turning to faith in Jesus at this time, led by Jewish people who supernaturally receive the revelation that *Yeshua*, Jesus, is the promised Messiah and go out with great power to preach the Gospel in the first half of the Great Tribulation. Because of the insecurity of the time and the fear in the hearts of many people this will be a very fruitful time for evangelism and as a result a huge number of people will come to faith:

> *'After these things I looked, and behold, a great multitude which no one could number, of all nations, tribes, peoples, and tongues, standing before the throne and before the Lamb, clothed with white robes, with palm branches in their hands, and crying out with a loud voice, saying, "Salvation belongs to our God who sits on the throne, and to the Lamb!"'*
>
> (Revelation 7:9–10)

For the most part these people will be martyred for their faith, as the persecutions of the Great Tribulation get under way (the main reason why we could not publish a book like this at that time!):

> *'When He opened the fifth seal, I saw under the altar the souls of those who had been slain for the word of God and for the testimony, which they held. And they cried with a loud voice, saying, "How long, O Lord, holy and true, until You judge and avenge our blood on those who dwell on the earth?"'*
>
> (Revelation 6:9–10)

> *'Then one of the elders answered, saying to me, "Who are these arrayed in white robes, and where did they come from?" And I said to him, "Sir, you know." So he said to me, "These are the ones who come out of the great tribulation, and washed their robes and made them white in the blood of the Lamb."'*
>
> (Revelation 7:13–14)

The majority of people however will not turn to Jesus Christ but to Antichrist. At the beginning of the tribulation section of the Book of Revelation we read of the famous 'Four Horsemen of the Apocalypse'.

> '*Now I saw when the Lamb opened one of the seals; and I*
> *heard one of the four living creatures saying with a voice like*
> *thunder, "Come and see." And I looked, and behold, a white*
> *horse. And he who sat on it had a bow; and a crown was*
> *given to him, and he went out conquering and to conquer.*
> *When He opened the second seal, I heard the second living*
> *creature saying, "Come and see." And another horse, fiery*
> *red, went out. And it was granted to the one who sat on it to*
> *take peace from the earth, and that people should kill one*
> *another; and there was given to him a great sword. When He*
> *opened the third seal, I heard the third living creature say,*
> *"Come and see." And I looked, and behold, a black horse,*
> *and he who sat on it had a pair of scales in his hand. And I*
> *heard a voice in the midst of the four living creatures saying,*
> *"A quart of wheat for a denarius, and three quarts of barley*
> *for a denarius; and do not harm the oil and the wine." When*
> *He opened the fourth seal, I heard the voice of the fourth*
> *living creature saying, "Come and see." And I looked, and*
> *behold, a pale horse. And the name of him who sat on it was*
> *Death, and Hades followed with him. And power was given to*
> *them over a fourth of the earth, to kill with sword, with*
> *hunger, with death, and by the beasts of the earth.'*
>
> (Revelation 6:1–8)

These verses show a sequence of events: the conquest of
the rider on the white horse, the red horse bringing war, the
black horse bringing famine and the pale horse bringing
death. This is an overview of the events that are to follow in
the Great Tribulation. The question is 'Who is the rider on
the white horse?' Some interpreters say this is Jesus riding out
to conquer with the Gospel, but there are objections to this
view. Firstly Jesus, glorified in heaven, is the one who is
revealing these things, not the one being revealed. Secondly
what follows the rider on the white horse is war, famine and
death, not what one associates with Good News (Gospel
means 'good news')!

Thirdly there is an interesting difference between the word
for 'crown' in this passage and the word for 'crown' in

Revelation 19:12 where the rider on the white horse most definitely is Jesus coming back as King of kings and Lord of lords. In Revelation 19:12 the word is 'diadem', the crown given from above to one who has royalty. It implies that he is the king by royal status and no matter what opinion anyone else may have of him it does not affect the fact that he is king. This clearly applies to Jesus. In Revelation 6:2, the 'Four Horsemen of the Apocalypse' passage, the crown is the Greek word *'stephanos'* which is the kind of crown given by popular approval to a victor at the games, or a victor in battle. This crown is given from below by the people to the man of their choice.

In this case the rider on the white horse is not Jesus Christ, but Antichrist, the one who comes with popular approval with his own agenda and in his own name claiming to be the Messiah for our time. He comes on a white horse indicating two things:

1. He is a counterfeit Christ or Messiah.
2. He comes with an offer of peace, which gives him popular approval.

As we have already seen the stage is being set for humanity to accept this one on both of these counts. Today there is an idea present that Christianity has failed, that Jesus may have been a Messiah for his time, but not **the** Messiah for all time and that with the vastly changing circumstances of our world we need a new Messiah for our time. Jesus prophesied that there would be false Messiahs and false prophets at the time of his second coming, who would lead many astray:

> *'Then if anyone says to you, "Look, here is the Christ [Messiah]!" or "There!" do not believe it. For false christs and false prophets will rise and show great signs and wonders, so as to deceive, if possible, even the elect. See, I have told you beforehand. Therefore if they say to you, "Look, He is in the desert!" do not go out; or "Look, He is in the inner rooms!" do not believe it. For as the lightning comes from the*

*east and flashes to the west, so also will the coming of the Son
of Man be.'*   (Matthew 24:23–27)

The Antichrist, with the vast communications network of
the world at his disposal, will have a power of persuasion
backed up by demonic signs and wonders which will dazzle
the minds of unbelievers:

*'And then the lawless one will be revealed, whom the Lord
will consume with the breath of His mouth and destroy with
the brightness of His coming. The coming of the lawless one is
according to the working of Satan, with all power, signs, and
lying wonders, and with all unrighteous deception among
those who perish, because they did not receive the love of the
truth, that they might be saved. And for this reason God will
send them a strong delusion, that they should believe the lie,
that they all may be condemned who did not believe the truth
but had pleasure in unrighteousness.'*

(2 Thessalonians 2:8–12)

The main fear of people alive at this time will be that a
world war using weapons of mass destruction will bring
about the end of the world. The fact that the rider comes
on a white horse indicates that he comes with a peace
programme, which gives him tremendous popular approval.
In 1 Thessalonians there is an indication that at this time
there is a great 'peace' movement taking place:

*'But concerning the times and the seasons, brethren, you have
no need that I should write to you. For you yourselves know
perfectly that the day of the Lord so comes as a thief in the
night. For when they say, "Peace and safety!" then sudden
destruction comes upon them, as labour pains upon a
pregnant woman.'*   (1 Thessalonians 5:1–3)

This global peace movement led by the Antichrist will offer
people a false security and will be the reason why he will be
accepted as world leader. He will not come conquering like

Hitler or Saddam Hussein by war, but offering what people desperately want – a peace process backed by a global power able to enforce it.

At the moment we see many preparations being made for this. As stated in Chapters 3 and 4 the world is coming together in the search for a global solution to global problems. As yet we do not see the UN with the kind of powers necessary to enforce the peace on warring regions of the world, but we do see progress being made in this direction. We also see nation states surrendering their sovereignty to regional blocs, particularly in the European Union.

The crisis, which is coming, will speed up this process and it will be presented to the people of the world as the only solution to the threat of mass destruction. People will be persuaded to surrender some personal liberties in order to survive and all the means of communication will be mobilised to put this message across. Dissenting views will be suppressed and the control systems described in Chapter 3 – video cameras, surveillance equipment, microchips, etc. – will be put to use by the emerging world government to track down opposition to its authority.

The issue which will cause the worldwide crisis of the end times will be the Arab-Israeli conflict and the question of who rules Jerusalem. Already this is the main area of world concern with more UN resolutions being passed on this issue than any other trouble spot on earth. For religious, economic and political reasons this crisis will focus the minds of the whole world in the last days and the search for a peace settlement will be of prime importance to the emerging world government.

It is likely that just prior to this there will be a limited Middle East war, which will threaten to go nuclear, but both sides will step back from the brink. In Chapters 7 and 8 we looked at the current line up against Israel and the reference in Psalm 83 to the surrounding nations wanting to eliminate Israel. We also saw how there has already been an attempt to arrange a 'seven year' peace plan for the region in the Oslo Accords, which broke down seven years after the treaty was signed. Another attempt to eliminate Israel, probably in fulfilment of Psalm 83, resulting again in failure for the Arab cause, would be enough to send the nations racing to the conference table to work out a settlement, especially if there has been the threat of nuclear weapons being used.

Prophecies in the book of Daniel indicate that the coming Antichrist will be the one who makes this peace settlement. As we have already seen in Chapter 8, in Daniel 9 we read of the *'prince who is to come'* who is the Antichrist, a figure associated with the Romans, the ones who destroyed the Second Temple:

> *'And after the sixty-two weeks*
> *Messiah shall be cut off, but not for Himself;*
> *And the people of the prince who is to come*
> *Shall destroy the city and the sanctuary.*
> *The end of it shall be with a flood,*
> *And till the end of the war desolations are*
> *   determined.*
> *Then he shall confirm a covenant with many*
> *   for one week;*
> *But in the middle of the week*
> *He shall bring an end to sacrifice and offering.*
> *And on the wing of abominations shall be one*
> *   who makes desolate,*
> *Even until the consummation, which is determined,*
> *Is poured out on the desolate.'*   (Daniel 9:26–27)

'One week' here is a seven-year period and this passage indicates a peace covenant made with many in Israel which will be the subject of a double-cross resulting in it being broken half way through (i.e. after $3\frac{1}{2}$ years). Daniel 11 indicates that the covenant being worked out will be based on deceit:

> *'And in his place shall arise a vile person, to whom they will not give the honour of royalty; but he shall come in **peace-ably**, and seize the kingdom by **intrigue**.'*   (Daniel 11:21)

> *'Both these kings' hearts shall be bent on evil, and they shall*
> *speak lies at the same table; but it shall not prosper, for the*
> *end will still be at the appointed time.'* (Daniel 11:27)

Through a mixture of promises of peace and deceit the
Antichrist will succeed in persuading Israel and the Arab
nations to make a peace settlement which will actually leave
him with the controlling power over Jerusalem. Those
making this settlement from Israel's side are described in
Isaiah 28 as *'scornful men'*. It is interesting that the Israeli
leaders like Shimon Peres and Yossi Beilin who have been
the driving force in the Oslo Agreement are 'scornful' of the
promises given by God for Israel in the Bible:

> *'Therefore hear the word of the* LORD,
>   *you scornful men,*
> *Who rule this people who are in Jerusalem,*
> *Because you have said, "We have made a*
>   *covenant with death,*
> *And with Sheol we are in agreement.*
> *When the overflowing scourge passes through,*
> *It will not come to us,*
> *For we have made lies our refuge,*
> *And under falsehood we have hidden ourselves."*
> *Therefore thus says the Lord* GOD:
> *"Behold, I lay in Zion a stone for a foundation,*
> *A tried stone, a precious cornerstone,*
>   *a sure foundation;*
> *Whoever believes will not act hastily.*
> *Also I will make justice the measuring line,*
> *And righteousness the plummet;*
> *The hail will sweep away the refuge of lies,*
> *And the waters will overflow the hiding place.*
> *Your covenant with death will be annulled,*
> *And your agreement with Sheol will not stand;*
> *When the overflowing scourge passes through,*
> *Then you will be trampled down by it.*
> *As often as it goes out it will take you;*

For morning by morning it will pass over,
And by day and by night;
It will be a terror just to understand the report."'

(Isaiah 28:14–19)

This *'covenant with death'* will be made by Israel to gain protection from *'the overflowing scourge'*, the threat of invasion and annihilation. However, it will not stand because it is based on lies and falsehood. The phrase *'the waters will overflow the hiding place'* points to the very thing Israel feared happening, an enemy invasion and occupation. This will lead to the final event in the tribulation, Armageddon, which will cause the *'report'* (the news) to be terrible.

In both the prophecy of Daniel 9:27 and Isaiah 28:14–19 there are those who do not enter into this false peace covenant. In Daniel 9 the Antichrist makes the covenant with *'some'* but not all. In Isaiah 28:16 there are those who do not act rashly but put their trust in God who says: *'Behold I lay in Zion a stone for a foundation, a tried stone, a precious corner stone, a sure foundation.'* This is a reference to Psalm 118:22, a Messianic Psalm which says,

'The stone which the builders rejected
Has become the chief cornerstone.
This was the LORD's doing;
It is marvellous in our eyes.'

This verse is used to point to Jesus as Messiah in the New Testament more than any other Old Testament scripture. It occurs in all four Gospels, in the Acts and in 1 Peter.

There is a story relating to this verse that as the builders were putting the great hewn stones of Solomon's Temple in place, they came across a stone, which was an odd shape and did not fit anywhere. So they rejected it and put it on the rubbish heap. As they came to the end of their building they found that there was an odd shaped space at the head of the corner. One of the builders who had been there at the beginning of the work remembered the odd shaped stone and they looked on the rubbish heap and found it. It was a perfect fit for the odd shaped space they had left at the head of the corner.

This story has an amazing message in relation to the messianic claim of Jesus. When he came the first time, for many Jewish people he did not fit the idea of Messiah and he was put on the rubbish heap spiritually and rejected. At the end of days as the final conflict rages around Jerusalem the remnant of Jewish people there will look upon *'him whom they have pierced and mourn for him as for an only Son'* (Zechariah 12:10). They will understand that he is the only one who can fit the empty space in their lives and fulfil their hopes of the Messiah. Then he will return and take up his place of honour and deliver Israel from destruction and create world peace.

Chapter 10

The Mark of the Beast

Although the Antichrist offers the world *'peace and safety'* he cannot deliver on this promise. *'Sudden destruction'* comes in many forms.

God himself sends judgement on the Antichrist world system because of its rejection of the true Messiah, Jesus, and its persecution and killing of those who believe in him. Revelation 8–9 describes the seven 'trumpet' judgements, as a result of which one third of the trees and green grass are burned up, a third of the creatures in the sea are killed as a *'great mountain burning with fire'* (asteroid?) is cast into the sea, a third of the freshwater on earth becomes bitter and undrinkable and there is a darkness covering the sun, moon and stars for a third of the day and night. All of these events actually tie up with fears people have today of the consequences of environmental damage to the earth. Whether this is the reason for these judgements coming or they are simply acts of God remains to be seen. Despite the fearsome nature of these events and the warning of worse to come, the majority of people harden their hearts against God and refuse to turn to him.

There is also rebellion within the camp. For reasons already stated the most likely geographic area for the Antichrist to come to power is the European area. This is also quite possible from the point of view of current events. Although the USA is the dominant superpower at the time of writing, there are many indications that American power could be on the wane. America is very unpopular in much of the world, including Europe and the Middle East. A terrorist attack on America or an intervention in the 'War on Terror' going wrong could bring the decline of US power. America is also hugely in debt with a vastly inflated economy, which could come crashing down.

Already European leaders are speaking of Europe as the next superpower. Its geographic position means it can act as a bridge between Russia and America. It also has links to the Middle East across the Mediterranean and overland via Turkey. It faces Africa, the area most in need of help in the world today. The European area is also situated on the territory of the old Roman Empire. It is the most advanced area in the world in the globalisation process of nation states surrendering sovereignty to a 'supra national' entity, which appears to be the global pattern for the last days.

The prophecies, as we have seen, indicate that the antichrist system will come in peaceably offering to save the world not to destroy it. Many European political leaders (including Tony Blair) have idealistic views on how a united Europe can bring peace and aid to needy parts of the world, especially Africa and the Middle East.

We have also noted in Chapter 4 that the Antichrist system comes in with the backing of ten kings:

> *'The ten horns which you saw are ten kings who have received no kingdom as yet, but they receive authority for one hour as kings with the beast. These are of one mind, and they will give their power and authority to the beast.'*
>
> (Revelation 17:12–13)

This indicates that these kings will voluntarily hand over their power to the Antichrist. Most likely this will be through some kind of emergency cabinet being set up at the UN to deal with the global crisis described in the previous chapter, as a result of which a single world government will be set up and led by the Antichrist. This will also be backed by an ecclesiastical power, which will unite all the religions. We will look in more detail at what will happen to this power in the next chapter. Both the political and the religious aspects of this administration will be strongly anti-Christian and will persecute true believers in Jesus.

Although the Antichrist will be granted worldwide authority, this will quickly break down and lead to the wars of the tribulation. The red horse will ride out with catastrophic results, leading to one-quarter of the earth's population being killed. In the book of Daniel we have further information about the ten kings which shows that three of them will rebel against the Antichrist:

> *'The ten horns are ten kings*
> *Who shall arise from this kingdom.*
> *And another shall rise after them;*
> *He shall be different from the first ones,*
> *And shall subdue three kings.'*   (Daniel 7:24)

In the book of Ezekiel we have a prophecy concerning the War of Gog and Magog, which will come in the last days, after the Jewish people are regathered to the land of Israel. In this prophecy the attack on Israel is led by a great power to the uttermost north:

> *'Son of man, set your face against Gog, of the land of Magog, the prince of Rosh, Meshech, and Tubal, and prophesy against him, and say, "Thus says the Lord GOD: 'Behold, I am against you, O Gog, the prince of Rosh, Meshech, and Tubal. I will turn you around, put hooks into your jaws, and lead you out, with all your army, horses, and horsemen, all splendidly clothed, a great company with bucklers and shields, all of them handling swords. Persia, Ethiopia, and Libya are with them, all of them with shield and helmet; Gomer and all its troops; the house of Togarmah from the far north and all its troops – many people are with you. Prepare yourself and be ready, you and all your companies that are*

gathered about you; and be a guard for them. After many days you will be visited. In the latter years you will come into the land of those brought back from the sword and gathered from many people on the mountains of Israel, which had long been desolate; they were brought out of the nations, and now all of them dwell safely. You will ascend, coming like a storm, covering the land like a cloud, you and all your troops and many peoples with you.'"'   (Ezekiel 38:2–9)

There are different views on how this passage fits in with the end time scriptures. Some say it happens before the Great Tribulation, others that it is the same as Armageddon. However, there are problems with it being the same as Armageddon. Firstly the Ezekiel passage has some countries in the world participating while others stand aside (see verse 13), whereas Armageddon involves all nations. Secondly the action takes place on the mountains of Israel, probably the Golan Heights, and does not appear to have any contact with Jerusalem, the main focus of Armageddon. Thirdly the armies are destroyed by an earthquake, *'flooding rain, great hailstones, fire, and brimstone'* (Ezekiel 38:19, 22), rather than by the person of the Messiah as at Armageddon.

It is also interesting that the army comes at a time when Israel is at peace (i.e. after a peace treaty has been signed and is working for a while). The nations referred to do not include any country which borders on Israel, unlike Psalm 83, which includes only countries bordering Israel plus Assyria (Iraq). So these countries have either made peace with Israel or been knocked out of the conflict in a previous war.

Identifying the actual countries referred to in Ezekiel 38 does present some problems, but it is clear that a great power to the uttermost north is mentioned. Go as far north as you can from Israel and you reach Russia. Moscow is almost due north of Jerusalem. Russia today is a reluctant ally with the West in the war on terror, but is also pursuing its own agenda in the Middle East, in particular making an alliance with one of the countries, which is clearly identified in Ezekiel 38, Iran or Persia.

While not wishing to be dogmatic on this question it has to be a possibility that this event is connected to the rebellion of the three kings against Antichrist's rule. Russia and the Muslim countries of the Middle East would certainly be very reluctant members of the global coalition and already feel humiliated and hostile to the west and to Israel. They would be key players in wanting to spoil the Antichrist's peace treaty over Israel.

According to Ezekiel's prophecy the defeat of this army is clearly an act of God and will be recognised as such by both Israel and the surrounding nations. For Islam it will be a devastating blow as it becomes finally apparent that God is not on their side. If the Dome of the Rock mosque is destroyed in the process this could lead to the possibility of the Temple being rebuilt in Jerusalem, with the Jewish people wanting to give thanks to God for their deliverance. There are already Jewish groups in Jerusalem planning the rebuilding of the Temple, making the necessary artefacts and training priests for animal sacrifices. The Antichrist who will be in power at the time could also sanction this project, but with his own sinister agenda in mind.

Daniel 11:40–45 also describes the wars, which the Antichrist will fight, resulting in him coming into Israel:

> *'And he shall plant the tents of his palace between the seas and the glorious holy mountain; yet he shall come to his end, and no one will help him.'* (Daniel 11:45)

The glorious holy mountain is the Temple Mount in Jerusalem and the seas are the Mediterranean and Dead Seas.

The Scriptures indicate that after the Antichrist has put down the rebellion against his rule at the midpoint of the tribulation period, he will have total control. This control will be given following an event which will cause the entire world to marvel and follow him:

> *'I saw one of his heads as if it had been mortally wounded, and his deadly wound was healed. And all the world marvelled and followed the beast. So they worshiped the*

dragon who gave authority to the beast; and they worshiped the beast, saying, "Who is like the beast? Who is able to make war with him?" And he was given a mouth speaking great things and blasphemies, and he was given authority to continue for forty-two months. Then he opened his mouth in blasphemy against God, to blaspheme His name, His tabernacle, and those who dwell in heaven. And it was granted to him to make war with the saints and to overcome them. And authority was given him over every tribe, tongue, and nation. And all who dwell on the earth will worship him, whose names have not been written in the Book of Life of the Lamb slain from the foundation of the world. If anyone has an ear, let him hear. He who leads into captivity shall go into captivity; he who kills with the sword must be killed with the sword. Here is the patience and the faith of the saints.'

(Revelation 13:3–10)

The event which causes this worship of the beast is *'his deadly wound'* being *'healed'*. What could this mean? There is much speculation on this but the most intriguing possibility is the one which comes closest to the literal interpretation of the text – that he experiences some kind of death and resurrection by the power of Satan (the dragon). Since we have already seen that he is a counterfeit Christ, what better way to convince the world that he is the Messiah than to counterfeit the resurrection of Jesus?

Whether or not this is the case, the result is clear. He is given absolute worldwide power over every nation on earth. People realise that any resistance to his power is futile as no one can make war with him and all dissenters who are caught face imprisonment or execution. The main source of opposition to his rule is the saints, those whose names are written in the Lamb's Book of Life, in other words true followers of Jesus. They are encouraged to hold firm to their faith, even if it means losing their lives as a result, because this period of tribulation is not going to last for long and the end result will be the persecutors being destroyed and the persecuted being saved.

His absolute power lasts for forty-two months, which is $3\frac{1}{2}$ years or half of the Great Tribulation period. This is Satan's finest hour, the goal towards which he has been working since the Garden of Eden. It will end in total defeat for him and the glorious 1,000 year reign of the true Messiah Jesus on the earth as a prelude to the eternal state in heaven. So the choice before people will be whether they want to be on the side of the loser who will have power for $3\frac{1}{2}$ years or on the side of the winner who will have power for eternity.

The choice will be a hard one to make because the Antichrist will then bring in a world system of control by which people will not be able to buy or sell unless they accept his authority and worship him. In this endeavour he will be helped by a second beast known as the False Prophet:

> *'Then I saw another beast coming up out of the earth, and he had two horns like a lamb and spoke like a dragon. And he exercises all the authority of the first beast in his presence, and causes the earth and those who dwell in it to worship the first beast, whose deadly wound was healed. He performs great signs, so that he even makes fire come down from heaven on the earth in the sight of men. And he deceives those who dwell on the earth by those signs which he was granted to do in the sight of the beast, telling those who dwell on the earth to make an image to the beast who was wounded by the sword and lived. He was granted power to give breath to the image of the beast, that the image of the beast should both speak and cause as many as would not worship the image of the beast to be killed. He causes all, both small and great, rich and poor, free and slave, to receive a mark on their right hand or on their foreheads, and that no one may buy or sell except one who has the mark or the name of the beast, or the number of his name. Here is wisdom. Let him who has understanding calculate the number of the beast, for it is the number of a man: His number is 666.'* (Revelation 13:11–18)

Here we see that the False Prophet will turn the worship of the Antichrist into a world religion, backed by deceiving supernatural signs and an act of amazing idolatry. An image is made of the Beast and people are given the choice of worshipping this image or being killed. With modern technology it is not impossible to see how such an image could be *'given breath'* and caused to speak. This act of idolatry will be coupled with the introduction of worldwide control of buying and selling. Those who worship the Beast will receive his mark, the famous 666, without which they will not be able to buy or sell. Again new technology has made this possible as we saw in Chapter 3.

There will be places people can flee to in order to escape this control system, which will be how there will be survivors of the Tribulation who will not take the mark of the beast. But this event will bring about the beginning of the most terrible time the world has ever known. Revelation 14:9–10 warns the world not to take the mark of the beast under any circumstances. Much better to be killed than to take this mark, which is a sign of submission to Satan and worship of his man on the earth:

> *'Then a third angel followed them, saying with a loud voice, "If anyone worships the beast and his image, and receives his mark on his forehead or on his hand, he himself shall also drink of the wine of the wrath of God, which is poured out full strength into the cup of His indignation. He shall be tormented with fire and brimstone in the presence of the holy angels and in the presence of the Lamb. And the smoke of their torment ascends forever and ever; and they have no rest day or night, who worship the beast and his image, and whoever receives the mark of his name." Here is the patience of the saints; here are those who keep the commandments of God and the faith of Jesus.'* (Revelation 14:9–12)

In Jesus' prophecy concerning the second coming he also warned about this event:

> *'Therefore when you see the 'abomination of desolation', spoken of by Daniel the prophet, standing in the holy place*

*(whoever reads, let him understand), then let those who are in
Judea flee to the mountains. Let him who is on the housetop
not come down to take anything out of his house. And let him
who is in the field not go back to get his clothes. But woe to
those who are pregnant and to those with nursing babies
in those days! And pray that your flight may not be in winter
or on the Sabbath. For then there will be great tribulation,
such as has not been since the beginning of the world until
this time, no, nor ever shall be. And unless those days were
shortened, no flesh would be saved; but for the elect's sake
those days will be shortened.'*   (Matthew 24:15–22)

The worship of the image of the beast is the same event as
the *'abomination of desolation'*. According to Jesus' prophecy
this triggers the events of the last of the last days and a time
of trouble so great that if God did not cut it short it would
bring all life on earth to an end. In Matthew 24 and in Daniel
11:31 the passage, which Jesus refers to in Matthew 24,
the focal point of the abomination, is *'the holy place'*, i.e. the
Temple Mount. This gives the reason for the Antichrist
permitting the rebuilding of the Temple in Jerusalem.

His aim was not for the Jewish people to give glory to the
God of Israel, but for his image to be placed there so he could
be worshipped in the holy place. There is a parallel to this
in the event which is also prophesied in Daniel 11, the
defilement of the Temple by Antiochus Epiphanes, in the
time of the Maccabees in 167 BC. This Gentile ruler defiled
the Temple by erecting an image to Zeus on the site and
sacrificing a pig there.

At this point the Jewish people will realise they have been
double-crossed by the Antichrist and will flee as instructed by
Jesus. They will go to a place prepared for them by God where
they will be kept safe until the second coming of the Messiah.

Following this the bowl judgements will be poured out on
the earth leading to the final battle of Armageddon:

*'Then the sixth angel poured out his bowl on the great river
Euphrates, and its water was dried up, so that the way of the*

kings from the east might be prepared. And I saw three unclean spirits like frogs coming out of the mouth of the dragon, out of the mouth of the beast, and out of the mouth of the false prophet. For they are spirits of demons, performing signs, which go out to the kings of the earth and of the whole world, to gather them to the battle of that great day of God Almighty. "Behold, I am coming as a thief. Blessed is he who watches, and keeps his garments, lest he walk naked and they see his shame." And they gathered them together to the place called in Hebrew, Armageddon.' (Revelation 16:12–16)

It is interesting that today the river Euphrates is at an all time low as a result of drought and dams placed by Turkey upstream. At places it is shallow enough to walk across. The great Antichrist peace programme unravels in most spectacular style with the armies of the world gathering together in the north of Israel in the plains of Megiddo, prior to the final battle which takes place at Jerusalem and brings back the Messiah Jesus to the earth. This event takes place just seven years after the peace covenant was made, just as the Oslo Accord, the dry run for the final conflict, broke down seven years after the covenant was signed.

Chapter 11

A Woman Rides the Beast

The prophecies in the Bible give a clear picture of what will happen in the religious world in the last days before Jesus returns. There is a positive and a negative side to this question.

Positive

The true church of Jesus Christ will be known to God and will make God known worldwide.

> 'Nevertheless the solid foundation of God stands, having this seal: "The Lord knows those who are His," and, "Let everyone who names the name of Christ depart from iniquity." '
>
> (2 Timothy 2:19)

> 'Then Jesus came and spoke to them, saying, "All authority has been given to Me in heaven and on earth. Go therefore and make disciples of all the nations, baptizing them in the name of the Father and of the Son and of the Holy Spirit, teaching them to observe all things that I have commanded you; and lo, I am with you always, even to the end of the age." '
>
> (Matthew 28:18–20)

Today we see that despite the opposition the message of the Gospel is going out to all the nations and that there are believers in Jesus in every nation. This does not mean that the nations will be 'christianised'. The true Church will be a minority saved by grace amidst a majority who are in rebellion against God, as we see from the following verses:

> *'Enter by the narrow gate; for wide is the gate and broad is the way that leads to destruction, and there are many who go in by it. Because narrow is the gate and difficult is the way which leads to life, and there are few who find it.'*
>
> (Matthew 7:13–14)

> *'Even so then, at this present time there is a remnant according to the election of grace.'*   (Romans 11:5)

The true Church will be saved from the wrath to come by the blood of Jesus and be caught up to meet him as he comes in the air:

> *'And they sang a new song, saying:*
>
> > *"You are worthy to take the scroll,*
> > *And to open its seals;*
> > *For You were slain,*
> > *And have redeemed us to God by Your blood*
> > *Out of every tribe and tongue and people and nation."'*
>
> (Revelation 5:9)

> *'For this we say to you by the word of the Lord, that we who are alive and remain until the coming of the Lord will by no means precede those who are asleep. For the Lord Himself will descend from heaven with a shout, with the voice of an archangel, and with the trumpet of God. And the dead in Christ will rise first. Then we who are alive and remain shall be caught up together with them in the clouds to meet the Lord in the air. And thus we shall always be with the Lord. Therefore comfort one another with these words.'*
>
> (1 Thessalonians 4:15–18)

Negative

As well as the true Church there is also an apostate church,
which comprises the majority of professing Christians. This
church denies the blood of Jesus as the only means whereby
sins are forgiven and is willing to make a compromise with
other faiths in an inter-faith union. This inter-faith union
will be known as Babylon, a false religious system, which will
cooperate with the coming Antichrist during the first half of
the Tribulation. He will use this religious system to gain
power.

> *'Then one of the seven angels who had the seven bowls came
> and talked with me, saying to me, "Come, I will show you the
> judgment of the great harlot who sits on many waters, with
> whom the kings of the earth committed fornication, and the
> inhabitants of the earth were made drunk with the wine of her
> fornication." So he carried me away in the Spirit into the
> wilderness. And I saw a woman sitting on a scarlet beast,
> which was full of names of blasphemy, having seven heads
> and ten horns. The woman was arrayed in purple and scarlet,
> and adorned with gold and precious stones and pearls, having
> in her hand a golden cup full of abominations and the
> filthiness of her fornication. And on her forehead a name
> was written:*
>
> > *MYSTERY, BABYLON THE GREAT,*
> > *THE MOTHER OF HARLOTS AND OF*
> > *THE ABOMINATIONS OF THE EARTH.*
>
> *And I saw the woman, drunk with the blood of the saints and
> with the blood of the martyrs of Jesus. And when I saw her, I
> marvelled with great amazement.'*   (Revelation 17:1–6)

This religious system is a whore (unfaithful) as opposed to
the faithful wife of Christ described in Revelation 19:7–9:

> *'"Let us be glad and rejoice and give Him glory, for the
> marriage of the Lamb has come, and His wife has made
> herself ready." And to her it was granted to be arrayed in fine*

> *linen, clean and bright, for the fine linen is the righteous acts of the saints. Then he said to me, "Write: 'Blessed are those who are called to the marriage supper of the Lamb!'" And he said to me, "These are the true sayings of God."'*

We have seen in the last chapter that during first half of the seven-year Great Tribulation period the beast or Antichrist is in power but not absolutely. During this time he rules in conjunction with ten kings, three of whom rebel against him. He also rules with the backing of the Babylon world religious system, a coming together of world faiths to try to save the world from disaster. We have already seen how global threats to the environment, fear of terrorism and other world crises are bringing nations and religions together in a search for a solution.

In Chapter 5 we saw how the religions of the world are coming together and how a false inter-faith union is becoming the accepted world religion. This form of religion already strongly opposes and ridicules the belief in the second coming of Christ (try passing this book around one of the great ecumenical or inter-faith gatherings).

During the first half of the Tribulation this religious system will persecute true believers in Jesus who will defy its message that all religions are the same. Because true Christians insist that only through faith in Jesus as Saviour and Lord can we be saved, the 'Babylon' world religion will brand them as 'fundamentalists' who are seen as the enemies of global harmony and therefore of humanity. 'Babylon' will be promoting a religion with New Age/occult leanings, which will be 'tolerant' of any lifestyle and belief, but intolerant of true believers in Jesus. Backed by the media, educational system, and the government, this religious organisation will support the Antichrist in his rise to absolute power.

A point, which is often missed by Bible commentators is that midway through the Tribulation period (i.e. after $3\frac{1}{2}$ years) there is a change in the way things are run by the Antichrist. The one world religious system of Babylon and the ten kings are the religious and political power base of Antichrist in first half of the Tribulation. But midway through several things happen. (Note the time period referred to in Daniel and Revelation – a time, times and half-a-time = $3\frac{1}{2}$ years [Daniel 7:25], half of seven years = $3\frac{1}{2}$ years [final 'week' of Daniel 9:27], 42 months = $3\frac{1}{2}$ years [Revelation 13:5], 1,260 days = $3\frac{1}{2}$ years [Revelation 12:6].)

At this point Satan comes down with great wrath:

> *'Then the woman fled into the wilderness, where she has a place prepared by God, that they should feed her there one thousand two hundred and sixty days. And war broke out in heaven: Michael and his angels fought against the dragon; and the dragon and his angels fought, but they did not prevail, nor was a place found for them in heaven any longer. So the great dragon was cast out, that serpent of old, called the Devil and Satan, who deceives the whole world; he was cast to the earth, and his angels were cast out with him. Then I heard a loud voice saying in heaven, "Now salvation, and strength, and the kingdom of our God, and the power of His Christ have come, for the accuser of our brethren, who accused them before our God day and night, has been cast down. And they overcame him by the blood of the Lamb and by the word of their testimony, and they did not love their lives to the death. Therefore rejoice, O heavens, and you who dwell in them! Woe to the inhabitants of the earth and the sea! For the devil has come down to you, having great wrath, because he knows that he has a short time."'*

(Revelation 12:6–12)

At the present time Satan is not seated on a fiery throne in hell with a pitchfork in his hand as he is sometimes colourfully presented. He is the *'prince of the power of the air'* ruling over the present evil in the world from his position between humanity and the throne of God. Before we believe in Jesus he is in a position above us and therefore controlling our thinking. Once we believe in Jesus the way is open for us to be above him, as we let God control our thinking and our lives. Paul describes this as being seated with Christ in heavenly places, far above Satan's rule (Ephesians 1:15–2:10).

At the mid point of the Tribulation Satan is cast out of his present position to the earth where he gives all power to his man on the earth, the Antichrist. This is the point at which the Antichrist has his counterfeit death and resurrection, which causes the world to marvel after him as we saw in the previous chapter. Then the False Prophet sets up the image of the beast to be worshipped. At this point there is a trinity of evil in control. The dragon (Satan) gives power to his man on earth (the Antichrist), who is borne witness to by the False Prophet. This is a counterfeit of the Father, Son and Holy Spirit. Satan always imitates God, and in this last act of desperation he wants to take the place of God on earth and be worshipped alone.

For this reason the beast turns on and eliminates Ecclesiastical Babylon. It is not just that he does not want true believers to worship God through Jesus the Messiah. He does not even want any remnant of worship of any god except himself. This is shown by a number of scriptures:

> '*Then the king shall do according to his own will: he shall exalt and magnify himself above every god, shall speak blasphemies against the God of gods, and shall prosper till the wrath has been accomplished; for what has been determined shall be done. He shall regard neither the God of his fathers nor the desire of women, nor regard any god; for he shall magnify himself above them all.*'   (Daniel 11:36–37)

> '*Let no one deceive you by any means; for that Day will not come unless the falling away comes first, and the man of sin is revealed, the son of perdition, who opposes and exalts himself above all that is called God or that is worshipped, so that he sits as God in the temple of God, showing himself that he is God.*'   (2 Thessalonians 2:3–4)

> '*These will make war with the Lamb, and the Lamb will overcome them, for He is Lord of lords and King of kings; and those who are with Him are called, chosen, and faithful. Then*

he said to me, "The waters which you saw, where the harlot sits, are peoples, multitudes, nations, and tongues. And the ten horns, which you saw on the beast, these will hate the harlot, make her desolate and naked, eat her flesh and burn her with fire. For God has put it into their hearts to fulfil His purpose, to be of one mind, and to give their kingdom to the beast, until the words of God are fulfilled. And the woman whom you saw is that great city which reigns over the kings of the earth."'   (Revelation 17:14–18)

Note that in all these passages the beast turns on all religions, not just on Bible believing followers of Jesus. His aim is the elimination of all faiths and their replacement with a new Messiah who is to be worshipped by all and who is empowered by Satan with counterfeit miracles to impress people that he is indeed God.

It is interesting to note here that Hitler used apostate Christianity to climb to power. He gained the allegiance of the German churches and was happy to use unfaithful clerics to give him a kind of legitimacy (while genuine Bible believing Christians opposed him). Once in power his aim was to replace Christianity with a religious system based on German nationalism and pre-Christian paganism, ultimately leading to worship of himself. Saying *'Heil Hitler'* (Hail Hitler) with one arm raised is in itself an act of worship. Other types of the coming Antichrist like Stalin and Mao Tse Tung established a kind of religious cult around themselves, bringing violent opposition and persecution on members of all religions, as well as Bible believing followers of Jesus.

Another significant point is that amongst many people, especially the young, there is widespread turning away from all religion. The growing power of the occult and fascination with the demonic realm is softening people up worldwide for the final stage of the satanic programme which is the elimination of all religion, true and false, and its replacement with a religious system which involves direct worship of Satan through his man on the earth the beast directed by the false prophet (the satanic trinity). Although we see Islam as being very powerful in countries under its control, there is in fact a growing opposition to the abuse of power by the mullahs (Islamic clergy), especially in Iran. As the end time events unfold we can expect to see dramatic changes in the Islamic world.

God's purpose in all this is to cleanse the earth of false religion. The Lord Jesus will personally destroy the world political and religious system of the satanic trinity at his second coming with the Beast and the False Prophet being thrown straight into the lake of fire and Satan being bound for 1,000 years, during which time there will be a pure faith on the earth. He will return with the saints who have previously been taken in the rapture (Zechariah 14:5; Jude 14, Revelation 19:14) and he will resurrect those who have been put to death by the Antichrist during the Great Tribulation (Revelation 20:4). He will also resurrect all the saints (true believers) from the Old Testament days (Daniel 12:2). That means that if you believe in Jesus you have a very exciting future in store for you!

Chapter 12

A Future and a Hope

'For I know the thoughts that I think toward you, says the
LORD, thoughts of peace and not of evil, to give you a future
and a hope.' (Jeremiah 29:11)

When we look at current world events we have to recognise
that the outlook on the human level is gloomy. We can also
say that the prospect of the Great Tribulation coming is
hardly a pleasant one. However, as we have already seen Jesus
told the disciples, *'Now when these things* [i.e. the signs of his
coming] *begin to happen, look up and lift up your heads, because
your redemption draws near'* (Luke 21:28). As far as unbelievers
are concerned these things coming on the world are a sign of
approaching doom. As far as believers are concerned they are
a sign of approaching deliverance at the return of the Lord:

'For the Lord Himself will descend from heaven with a shout,
with the voice of an archangel, and with the trumpet of God.
And the dead in Christ will rise first. Then we who are alive
and remain shall be caught up together with them in the
clouds to meet the Lord in the air. And thus we shall always
be with the Lord.' (1 Thessalonians 4:16–17)

'Behold I tell you a mystery: We shall not all sleep, but we
shall all be changed – in a moment, in the twinkling of an

*eye, at the last trumpet. For the trumpet will sound, and the
dead will be raised incorruptible, and we shall be changed.
For this corruptible* [body] *must put on incorruption and this
mortal* [body] *must put on immortality.'*

(1 Corinthians 15:51–53)

This means that believers have the glorious prospect in
front of them of receiving a new body. I wonder how many
people reading this book feel that the older they get, the
better their bodies function. For most of us, once we get
beyond 25–30 as far as our bodies are concerned, it is
downhill all the way. The older we get, the more rapid the
decline, until eventually our bodies pack up altogether and
we die. If death is the end of our existence, this is a very
depressing prospect. We have our moment of pleasure and
achievement (perhaps) and then it is all over and within a
few years most people have forgotten us. Whether we are
high flyers, accomplishing great things in our lives, or live at
the bottom of the human pile, in the end it makes no
difference. Decline and death are the only certainty facing
us all. Or are they?

Well, according to these verses there is one generation
which will not see death, because they will be alive at
the time of the coming of the Lord. They will experience
a marvellous transformation at the event known as the
Rapture in which they suddenly receive a new body which
will never get sick or old or die, but will be perfect and able to
do things we could only dream of doing in these present
bodies. They will be caught up to meet the Lord in the air as
he comes. All those who died before this event will also be
resurrected and also receive a new body. So all believers will
be united with the Lord at this time.

This glorious future is only available to those who accept
Jesus as Saviour, so if you have not yet done so, now is the
time to take this step.

*'The time is fulfilled, and the kingdom of God is at hand.
Repent and believe in the gospel.'*   (Mark 1:15)

*'If you confess with your mouth the Lord Jesus and believe in
your heart that God raised Him from the dead, you will be
saved.'*   (Romans 10:9)

The following prayer is an invitation to accept Jesus as
Saviour:

Dear Heavenly Father, I admit that I am a sinner and
need your forgiveness. I believe that Jesus is the Messiah
who died in my place paying the penalty for my sins. I
ask you to forgive me for all the sins I have committed.
I am willing right now to accept the salvation, which
Jesus gained for me when he died on the cross and rose
again from the dead. I commit my life to you and ask
you to send the Holy Spirit into my life, to fill me and to
take control and to help me become the kind of person
you want me to be. Thank you, Father, for loving me. In
Jesus' name, Amen.

For those who do this, the future is so wonderful that it is
beyond the power of human words to describe or human
minds to comprehend:

'Eye has not seen, nor ear heard,
Nor have entered into the heart of man
The things which God has prepared for those who love
        Him.'   (1 Corinthians 2:9)

After Jesus has taken us, either in death or the Rapture, we
will appear before him:

'For we must all appear before the judgment seat of Christ,
that each one may receive the things done in the body,
according to what he has done, whether good or bad.'
                                        (2 Corinthians 5:10)

This is not a judgement for heaven or hell, but a judgement
of believers for rewards according to what we have done

while we were alive. Therefore we need to use the time that remains to us in this life to serve the Lord and to seek to win others to him.

This will be followed by the glorious reunion described in the Book of Revelation, the Marriage of the Lamb:

> *'And I heard, as it were, the voice of a great multitude, as the sound of many waters and as the sound of mighty thunderings, saying, "Alleluia! For the Lord God Omnipotent reigns! Let us be glad and rejoice and give Him glory, for the marriage of the Lamb has come, and His wife has made herself ready." And to her it was granted to be arrayed in fine linen, clean and bright, for the fine linen is the righteous acts of the saints. Then he said to me, "Write: 'Blessed are those who are called to the marriage supper of the Lamb!' "'*
>
> (Revelation 19:6–9)

This tremendous event will gather together all those who have trusted the Lord for the greatest celebration which has ever been known. This meeting takes place *'in the air'* (in other words not on the earth). But the next stage of the programme is the physical return of the Lord Jesus to the earth. He will not come alone but with all the believers:

> *'Then I saw heaven opened, and behold, a white horse. And He who sat on him was called Faithful and True, and in righteousness He judges and makes war ... He was clothed with a robe dipped in blood, and His name is called The Word of God. And the armies in heaven, clothed in fine linen, white and clean, followed Him on white horses.'*
>
> (Revelation 19:11–14)

Revelation 19:8 tells us that the *'fine linen is the righteous acts of the saints'* thus identifying this army with the believers in Jesus, as well as the angelic armies which will accompany the Lord. (NB: In the New Testament the word 'saint' means anyone who believes in Jesus as Saviour and Lord.)

The letter of Jude also tells us that the Lord is coming to the earth with his saints:

> 'Now Enoch, the seventh from Adam, prophesied about these men also, saying, "Behold, the Lord comes with ten thousands of His saints, to execute judgment on all, to convict all who are ungodly among them of all their ungodly deeds which they have committed in an ungodly way, and of all the harsh things which ungodly sinners have spoken against Him."'   (Jude 14–15)

Zechariah 14 is a parallel passage to this and tells us (verse 5) that the Lord will come with the saints at the height of a worldwide conflict over Jerusalem. This event will bring about a swift and sudden end to the satanic trinity:

> 'Now out of His mouth goes a sharp sword, that with it He should strike the nations. And He Himself will rule them with a rod of iron ... And I saw the beast, the kings of the earth, and their armies, gathered together to make war against Him who sat on the horse and against His army. Then the beast was captured, and with him the false prophet who worked signs in his presence, by which he deceived those who received the mark of the beast and those who worshipped his image. These two were cast alive into the lake of fire burning with brimstone.'   (Revelation 19:15, 19–20)

While the Beast and the False Prophet are thrown straight into the lake of fire, the dragon, Satan, is bound in a pit for a thousand years during which time he will be unable to deceive the nations (Revelation 19:20–20:3).

The believers who return with the Lord will reign with him in the Messianic kingdom or Millennium which follows. Those who turned to the Lord and refused the mark of the Beast during the Tribulation and were martyred for their faith will then be resurrected and also reign with Christ (Revelation 20:4), along with all Old Testament saints (Daniel 12:2). Those who survive the Tribulation period as believers and do not receive the mark of the Beast, will live on in their mortal bodies and have children in the normal way.

During this time God will demonstrate how the earth should be run. After the devastation caused by the Tribulation period, living waters will flow out from Jerusalem to clean up the earth (Zechariah 14:8). Weapons of war will be destroyed and all military training will cease:

> *'He shall judge between the nations*
> *And shall rebuke many people;*
> *They shall beat their swords into ploughshares,*
> *And their spears into pruning hooks;*
> *Nation shall not lift up sword against nation,*
> *Neither shall they learn war any more.'*　　　(Isaiah 2:4)

See also Isaiah 9:5 and Ezekiel 38:9.

The nations will go up to the redeemed Jerusalem where the Messiah Jesus will teach them the ways of the Lord. There will be universal peace and even the animal kingdom will be affected with meat eating creatures becoming vegetarian. The earth shall be full of the knowledge of the Lord as the waters cover the sea (Isaiah 11:6–9).

This glorious time will be a Sabbath of rest for the earth. If we take a literal view of creation and reckon the second coming of Christ to be not too far away, this gives about 6,000 years from creation to the end of this age. The Millennial period will last 1,000 years according to Revelation. In 2 Peter 3:8 we read that a day with the Lord is as 1,000 years. So we have a parallel with the creation account: six days of labour followed by the Sabbath day of rest; 6,000 years of travail and sin on the earth, followed by 1,000 years of rest and peace.

In this time Messiah Jesus will *'rule with a rod of iron'*, but also with absolute justice (Isaiah 11:4–5). The benefits will be obvious to all, especially those who have experienced the horrors of the Great Tribulation. Children will be born during this time in the natural way to survivors of the Great Tribulation who enter the Messianic kingdom. They will not have the opportunity to sin in the way we have today, Satan being bound and unable to influence the nations, and Jesus ruling with power on the earth.

However, the possibility of sin will be present during this time. In Isaiah 65:20 we read:

> *'No more shall an infant from there live*
> *but a few days,*
> *Nor an old man who has not fulfilled his days;*
> *For the child shall die one hundred years old,*
> *But the sinner being one hundred years old*
> *shall be accursed.'*

We also read of nations which refuse to worship the Lord during this time and suffer judgement as a result (Zechariah 14:17–19). At the end of the 1,000 year period Satan will be loosed for a while and gather together those who are inwardly rebelling against the rule of Christ:

> *'Now when the thousand years have expired, Satan will be released from his prison and will go out to deceive the nations which are in the four corners of the earth, Gog and Magog, to gather them together to battle, whose number is as the sand of the sea. They went up on the breadth of the earth and surrounded the camp of the saints and the beloved city. And fire came down from God out of heaven and devoured them. And the devil, who deceived them, was cast into the lake of fire and brimstone where the beast and the false prophet are. And they will be tormented day and night forever and ever.'*
> (Revelation 20:7–10)

This will actually be the last battle on earth, and like Armageddon, it will end in a moment with Satan's forces being routed. It will also be the end of the world, as this earth and everything in it will be destroyed and the final Day of Judgment before the great white throne of God takes place.

Zechariah speaks of the Feast of Tabernacles being celebrated during this time. The Feast of Tabernacles is a festival looking back to the time when the Israelites dwelt in booths after they came out of Egypt and before they came into the Promised Land. The booths represent a temporary dwelling place before the final destination, which God has prepared for his people. So the Millennium is a temporary dwelling place for those who have 'come out of Egypt' (symbolising the world system in rebellion against God) before entering into the final rest in heaven.

Revelation 19–21 gives a prophetic overview of the events of the end of the world which follows a logical sequence: the battle of Armageddon, the Second Coming of Christ to the earth, his rule for 1,000 years, Satan's loosing and rebellion at the end of the 1,000 years, the end of the world, heaven and hell.

After all this the physical universe in its present form will *'melt with fervent heat'* and the earth will be burnt up (2 Peter 3:10). The wicked dead will come before God in judgement:

> *'Then I saw a great white throne and Him who sat on it, from whose face the earth and the heaven fled away. And there was found no place for them. And I saw the dead, small and great, standing before God, and the books were opened. And another book was opened, which is the Book of Life. And the dead were judged according to their works, by the things which were written in the books. The sea gave up the dead who were in it, and Death and Hades delivered up the dead who were in them. And they were judged, each one according to his works. Then Death and Hades were cast into the lake of fire. This is the second death. And anyone not found written in the Book of Life was cast into the lake of fire.'*

(Revelation 20:11–15)

While many try to avoid the subject, the Bible is clear that hell exists. It is a place of absolute separation from God for eternity. Jesus made it clear that nothing is more important than making sure we avoid this place of torment:

> *'Do not fear those who kill the body, but cannot kill the soul.*
> *But rather fear Him who is able to destroy both soul and body*
> *in hell.'*   (Matthew 10:28)

People often ask, 'How can a loving God send people to hell?' In fact God has done all that he can to save us from hell. According to his justice he must punish sin. In his love and mercy the Lord Jesus left heaven and became man. He lived a perfect life without sin and then endured the punishment we deserve by dying for us on the cross. Being the sinless Son of God his sacrifice was accepted by the Father, so that all who repent (turn from sin) and believe in Jesus as Saviour and Lord are born again of the Holy Spirit, so receiving eternal life.

> *'For God so loved the world that He gave His only begotten*
> *Son, that whoever believes in Him should not perish but have*
> *everlasting life ... He who believes in the Son has everlasting*
> *life; and he who does not believe the Son shall not see life, but*
> *the wrath of God abides on him.'*   (John 3:16, 36)

The eternal one became sin and experienced hell for a moment in order that we could be saved from hell for eternity. It is not God who sends people to hell as much as we who send ourselves there if we refuse to accept this great sacrifice he has made for us.

Another common question asked about this subject is, 'How will God judge those who have never heard the Gospel?' Paul's letter to the Romans chapter 1 makes it clear that there is a general revelation of the nature of God available in the created universe:

> *'For since the creation of the world His invisible attributes are*
> *clearly seen, being understood by the things that are made,*
> *even His eternal power and Godhead, so that they are without*
> *excuse.'*   (Romans 1:20)

There is also the witness of our own conscience and moral values in the judgements we make of others:

'Therefore you are inexcusable, O man, whoever you are who judge, for in whatever you judge another you condemn yourself; for you who judge practice the same things.'

(Romans 2:1)

Someone once pointed out that if a tape recording were played back to us on the Day of Judgement of all the things we judge and criticise others for alongside a review of our own lives, we would all be condemned out of our own mouths!

One thing we can be sure of is that God will be perfectly fair and just in his dealings with those who have not heard the Gospel. But if you have read this book so far and not yet made a decision for Jesus you have heard the Gospel so this is not an excuse that you can make! As the writer to the Hebrews puts it:

'How shall we escape if we neglect so great a salvation?'

(Hebrews 2:3)

Those who are saved through putting their trust in Jesus as Saviour and Lord enter into eternal life in Heaven. Here at last we will experience eternal deliverance from the troubles and pains of this life. Heaven will not end in failure as all the ages of this world have ended in failure, because of human sinfulness and satanic activity. Only the Lord will be present there and all those who have been redeemed. Satan and those who have rejected this redemption will be unable to enter.

In the presence of the Lord the redeemed will have full unbroken fellowship with God, which we can never achieve on earth because of the weakness of human nature. We will have new bodies, which will never get old, sick or die (1 Corinthians 15). We will also be recognisable to those who have known us and will preserve our identity. Human relationships will not be on the same basis as on earth. There is no marriage in Heaven for example (Luke 20:37–38). Because there is no death there is no need for a new generation to replace the old. But fellowship between the redeemed will be more wonderful than anything we have ever experienced on earth. The bond of love in Heaven is stronger than the strongest bonds on earth.

In God's presence is fullness of joy. No one is ever sad in Heaven. None of the things that cause unhappiness on earth can enter Heaven. There is no unkindness, no cruelty, no selfishness, no loneliness, no misunderstanding.

> *'And God will wipe away every tear from their eyes; there shall be no more death, nor sorrow, nor crying; and there shall be no more pain, for the former things have passed away.'*
> (Revelation 21:4)

See you there?

Appendix 1

The Rapture and the Millennium

I spend a lot of my time travelling around the country speaking on issues relating to the end times. I can almost guarantee that after such a talk someone will come up to me and say, 'We never hear about this in our church.' Perhaps one reason why many pastors do not like to speak about this issue is that they know that there will probably be a number of different views on the subject in the church and they do not want to create controversy. But Jesus was never bothered about creating controversy and if we neglect the subject for this reason, we have given Satan the victory and have to ignore a large amount of the Bible!

The two major issues which divide Christians are the Rapture of the Church and the Millennium. The questions are:

1. 'Will the believing Church go through the Great Tribulation or be taken out before it begins?'
2. 'Will there be a literal 1,000 year reign of Jesus Christ on the earth after his second coming?'

The Rapture

I have already raised this question in Chapter 9. The point at issue is, 'Does the Rapture of the Church described in 1 Thessalonians 4:16–17 coincide with the coming of the

Lord to the earth or is it separated in time by a period of years?' In the most common understanding of this view, the period in question is seven years. In other words, 'Is the Second Coming of Christ in two stages?'

The view that the second coming is in two stages is known as the pre-Tribulation rapture, because this event is said to precede the final seven years of the Great Tribulation described in Matthew 24:15–31 and in Revelation 6–19. Critics of this view say that the second coming is all one event and that the idea of a separation in time between the two stages of the second coming is a 'novel idea', which the early Church knew nothing of.

The usual criticism is that the pre-Tribulation rapture theory originated around 1820, ascribed either to Emmanuel Lacunza (1812), Edward Irving (1816), Margaret Macdonald (1830) or John Darby (1820). Dave MacPherson in *The Incredible Cover Up* stated:

> Margaret Macdonald was the first person to teach a coming of Christ that would precede the days of Antichrist. Before 1830 Christians had always believed in a single future coming, that the catching up of 1 Thessalonians 4 will take place after the Great Tribulation of Matthew 24 at the glorious coming of the Son of Man when He shall send His angels to gather together all of His elect.

However, there is evidence of an understanding of the coming of the Lord in two stages in the early Church. I am not claiming that this proves the case, but it does show that this is not just an idea which has been around only from the 19th century onwards. The writer Ephraem the Syrian was a major theologian of the early Byzantine Church. He lived from 306 to 373. In his work *On the Last Times, the Antichrist and the End of the World*, he wrote:

> For all the saints and elect of God are gathered prior to the tribulation that is to come, and are taken to the Lord

lest they see the confusion that is to overwhelm the world because of our sins.

Ephraem's text shows a literal method of interpreting Scripture and teaches the pre-millennial return of Christ. It reveals a clear statement about the Lord returning before the Tribulation to take his elect saints home to be with him to escape the coming Tribulation. In addition Ephraem declares his belief in a personal Antichrist who will rule the Roman Empire during the last days, a rebuilt Temple, the two witnesses and a literal Great Tribulation lasting 1,260 days.

Ephraem's writing concludes:

> And there will be a great tribulation, as there has not been since people began to be on the earth ... and no one is able to sell or buy of the grain of the harvest, unless he is the one who has the serpentine sign on the forehead or the hand. And when the three and a half years have been completed, the time of the Antichrist, through which he will have seduced the world, after the resurrection of the two prophets, in the hour which the world does not know and on the day which the enemy or the son of perdition does not know, will come the sign of the Son of Man, and coming forward the Lord shall appear with great power and much majesty, with the sign of salvation going before him, and also even with all the powers of the heavens with the whole chorus of the saints.

So the teaching that the second coming is in two stages was not unknown to the early Church. It may have been little known and understood, but that is not a bar to it being true. At the time of the first coming of the Messiah Jesus, it was not understood even by his closest disciples that there were to be two stages in his Messianic mission, the first to suffer and die as a sacrifice for sin (in fulfilment of prophecies such as Isaiah 53), the second to rule and reign over the redeemed earth (in fulfilment of Isaiah 2:1–4 and other prophecies). After the Day of Pentecost they understood the truth that there was to be a time gap between his first and second coming during which time they were to evangelise the world (see Acts 1:6–8).

The literal understanding of the prophecies also demands that there is a time gap between the first and second stage of the second coming of Christ. The first stage, the Rapture of the Church, happens unexpectedly, as a thief in the night. Even from the point of view of the writers of the New Testament it could happen at any time:

> *'You also be patient. Establish your hearts, for the coming of the Lord is at hand.'*   (James 5:8)

See also 1 Corinthians 1:7; 16:22; 1 Thessalonians 1:10; Titus 2:13; Hebrews 9:28; 1 Peter 1:13; Jude 21 and Revelation 3:11; 22:7, 12, 17, 20.

If the rule of Antichrist, the Great Tribulation and the Mark of the Beast system had to come first it would be impossible for Christ to come at any time as was the expectation of the early Christians.

In 1 Thessalonians 5:3, people are saying *'Peace and safety!'* at the time of the Lord coming as a *'thief in the night'*. They will hardly be saying this after all the plagues of Revelation have been poured out and as the armies of the world gather at Armageddon. Also if you take the times given in Daniel and Revelation literally you should be able to work out the date of the second coming, something Jesus says we cannot do. Once you get to the peace treaty being signed with Israel you know there are seven years to go. Once you get to the Mark of the Beast system being set up worldwide you know there are $3\frac{1}{2}$ years to go.

Expecting Jesus to come at any time means that we as believers should keep our lives in continual readiness for this event as John taught in his epistle:

> *'We know that when He is revealed, we shall be like Him, for we shall see Him as He is. And everyone who has this hope in Him purifies himself, just as He is pure.'*   (1 John 3:2–3)

This is also a tremendous hope for those who are suffering in this body:

> *'For our citizenship is in heaven, from which we eagerly wait*
> *for the Saviour, the Lord Jesus Christ, who will transform our*
> *lowly body that it may be conformed to His glorious body . . .*
> *The Lord is at hand.'*   (Philippians 3:20–21; 4:5)

One further point is that according to 1 Thessalonians 5:9 *'God has not appointed us to wrath but unto salvation'*. The Great Tribulation can be seen as the time of God's wrath against an unbelieving world, as opposed to general tribulation which believers endure because of the hostility of Satan to true followers of Jesus. Since we have been saved from the wrath of God by believing in Jesus, God rescues his people before pouring out his wrath on the world, as he did with Lot and his family before judgement fell on Sodom.

The Millennium

The controversy about the Millennium centres on the question of Chapter 20 in the Book of Revelation and a number of passages in the Old Testament. The word Millennium is in fact taken from two Latin words, *'mille'*, meaning '1,000' and *'annus'*, meaning 'year'. According to Revelation 20 this is the 1,000 year period when Satan will be bound (unable to influence the world) and Jesus will reign on the earth (along with true believers who will be resurrected at this time):

> *'Blessed and holy is he who has part in the first resurrection.*
> *Over such the second death has no power, but they shall be*
> *priests of God and of Christ, and shall reign with Him a*
> *thousand years.'*   (Revelation 20:6)

There are also a number of Old Testament passages which deal with this subject, notably Psalms 2 and 72; Isaiah 2:1–4; 11–12; Ezekiel 40–48; Daniel 7:13–14 and Zechariah 14.

According to these passages Messiah will come in the clouds of heaven with all the power of God at his disposal to destroy all that opposes his rule. All international conflicts will cease and there will be world peace in which even the animal kingdom will be at peace with itself. His dominion will reach to the ends of the earth and all nations will come up to worship him and learn from him at the rebuilt Temple in Jerusalem. Israel will be regathered and at last know peace and safety as Jewish people recognise *Yeshua* (Jesus) as the promised Messiah.

The question is 'Should these passages be taken literally as events which will take place on earth, or are they allegorical of the life of the believing church on the earth now or of the future life in heaven?' The main views on this subject are known as 'pre-millennialism', 'a-millennialism' and 'post-millennialism'. Such words are no doubt a big turn-off to many, but it is not so difficult to understand them. 'Pre-millennialism' means that Jesus comes back 'pre' (before) the Millennium. 'Post-millennialism' means he comes back 'post' (after) it. 'A-millennialism' means there is no millennium ('a' is the Greek prefix meaning 'no'), but the prophecies about this are now happening symbolically through the Church.

Perhaps the main view in the Church today is 'a-millennialism'. For those who take this view the second coming is the end of the world and the beginning of heaven and hell. Therefore there is no time when Jesus reigns in person on the earth.

If one takes this line there are a number of passages in Scripture, which have to be taken allegorically rather than literally. For example the text in Isaiah 2:4 says, *'Nation shall not lift up sword against nation'*. Taken literally this means that there will be a time when conflicts between nations will cease. Clearly this has not happened since Jesus came the first time. For pre-millennialists this is not a problem because it will happen literally after the second coming. For a-millennialists it has to be interpreted symbolically. One way of looking at it is to point out that former enemies who come to faith in Jesus are often reconciled and become friends, rather than meaning that all conflict itself will cease. By this logic it can be said that this is happening now in situations where, for example, an Israeli and an Arab believer in Jesus have fellowship in the Lord.

According to this view the second coming itself seems to be a bit of a wasted journey – a walk through the ruins of a shattered world after the time of great tribulation, only to blow up the planet and make a new one. God could do this without Jesus having to leave heaven at all.

Another view is called 'post-millennialism' which means that the second coming happens after (post) the Church has succeeded in establishing the kingdom on the earth through a great revival which, it is claimed, will convert all the nations to Christianity.

Dave Mansell wrote in *Restoration Magazine*, January 1991:

> A new order is emerging in purity and power – the kingdom of God. The people of God, united in love and submission to Jesus Christ, will fill the earth as they take the kingdom and as all nations are brought beneath the feet of King Jesus.

John Giminez wrote in *New Wine Magazine*, January 1986:

> We believe it's God's will that the righteous should reign on this earth, and we're seeing people preparing themselves to be lawyers, doctors, generals, admirals, presidents, and congressmen. The righteous will rule and the people will rejoice.

The evidence of this happening on this side of the second coming of Christ is thin to say the least. Jesus taught in Matthew 13:24–43 that good and evil will coexist until the end of this age and according to Revelation 13 the second coming will be preceded by the vast majority of people turning to Antichrist not to Jesus Christ.

I believe the pre-millennial view, which means that Jesus

comes back pre (before) the Millennium. Jesus will come back in person to the earth at the time of the Great Tribulation, and then establish the glorious reign of the true Messiah, showing how the world should be run under God's authority.

The pre-millennial view was the expectation of the early Church, as is testified by a number of sources. Edward Gibbon (1737–1794), author of *The History of the Decline and Fall of the Roman Empire*, stated,

> The ancient and popular doctrine of the Millennium was intimately connected with the second coming of Christ ... It was inferred that this long period of labour and contention would be succeeded by a joyful Sabbath of 1,000 years; and that Christ, with the triumphant band of saints and the elect who had escaped death, or who had been miraculously revived, would reign upon earth till the time appointed for the last and general resurrection. Though it might not be universally received, it appears to have been the reigning sentiment of the orthodox believers.

Gibbon was a historian trying to uncover the facts and was not sympathetic to Christianity, so his comments do not come with any bias of his own belief.

In his writing *Dialogue with Trypho*, Justin Martyr, who lived from approximately 100 to 165 AD, stated,

> But I and others, who are right minded Christians on all points, are assured that there will be a resurrection of the dead, and a thousand years in Jerusalem, which will then be adorned, and enlarged as the prophets Ezekiel and Isaiah and others declare ... And further there was a certain man with us, whose name was John, one of the apostles of Christ, who prophesied, by a revelation that was made to him, that those who believed in our Christ would dwell one thousand years in Jerusalem; and that thereafter the general and in short the eternal resurrection and judgement of all men would take place.

Justin's use of the phrase 'right minded Christians on all points' indicates that this view of the Millennium was the prevailing one in his day. He also gives as his authority the Apostle John who was 'with us' (i.e. known to him).

This view began to lose influence in the third century of the Christian era with the teachings of the Greek theologian Origen who adopted an allegorical method of interpreting the prophets. In other words he taught that instead of speaking about a time when Jesus would literally rule the earth from Jerusalem and swords would be beaten into ploughshares, the prophecies indicate a spiritual kingdom in which Jesus would reign from heaven in the hearts of believers and there would be peace in their relationships with each other. One of Origen's disciples, called Dionysius, went so far in opposing the idea of a literal reign of Messiah on earth that he influenced the Greek Church to remove the Book of Revelation from the New Testament. It was not restored until the late Middle Ages.

The major influence on the Roman Church, Augustine, also rejected the idea of a literal reign of the Messiah on the earth. In his book *City of God* he wrote that the abyss into which Satan is cast in the Millennium (Revelation 20:1–3) is not a literal location. Instead he said,

> By the abyss is meant the countless multitude of the wicked whose hearts are unfathomably deep in malignity against the Church of God.

He said that the binding of Satan in the abyss 'means his being unable to seduce the church'. He was convinced that this binding of Satan in the abyss is a reality in this present Church age.

This teaching led into the rise of Roman Catholicism as the Church ruling and reigning for Jesus in this age and the Pope as the Vicar of Christ on earth enforcing His will (i.e. 'binding' or preventing the influence of evil). Unfortunately far from being 'unable to seduce the church', by the Middle Ages, Satan was more or less running the show, with the true

Gospel suppressed and real Christians ruthlessly persecuted, along with Jews and others who stood in the way of the so-called 'Church Triumphant'.

With the Reformation there came a renewed interest in studying the Bible, but end time prophecy was not high on the agenda of the Reformers. Many of them tended to take on board the Roman Catholic view that the Millennium should be applied to the spiritual reign of Christ in the Church, not a future event to take place after His second coming. That is why today belief in the literal Millennium remains a minority view among Christians.

Fortunately what will happen does not depend on what we believe, but on what God decrees. He is not going to let Satan have the last word in the affairs of this planet by making the reign of Antichrist and the Great Tribulation the end of the world. Rather, he will show through the glorious thousand year reign of the Messiah just how wonderful life on this planet can be when God, not Satan and human sin, are in control. This prelude to the eternal state (Revelation 21–22) is something to look forward to as the days of this age become darker and the forces of evil become stronger.

Satan will have his brief day in the coming Great Tribulation (seven years), but the Lord Jesus will rule and reign for 1,000 glorious years on earth and then for eternity in heaven. The choice to the human race is whether to join the loser in his eternal doom or to get on the winning side and believe in the Messiah who is coming again in triumph.

Appendix 2

Roman Catholicism and the Bible

Today we see the coming together of various Christian denominations through the activities of the Ecumenical Movement and the World Council of Churches. Even many evangelical Christians are now saying that there is no real difference in belief between Roman Catholics and Protestants and that the Reformation was a mistake. Those who say that there is a difference in belief are often condemned as 'unloving' and 'bigoted'. Roman Catholics who are said to 'believe the same as we do' are held up as proof that we all belong to the same faith.

It is not my purpose to be either unloving or bigoted and I do not wish to stir up hostility against Roman Catholics as people, since God loves them as he loves everyone. Nor am I doubting that many Roman Catholics are sincere in their faith. However, sincerity is not a guarantee of truth and it needs to be recognised that there are very significant errors in Roman Catholic teaching when looked at in the light of the Bible. Because of this those who have come to a saving faith in Jesus Christ within the Roman Catholic should leave it and join a Bible believing fellowship, as the Lord commands in Revelation 18:4, *'Come out of her my people, lest you share in her sins'*.

The reason for this is that Roman Catholicism and the Ecumenical Movement are bringing to birth the multi-faith apostate world religion described in Revelation 17. 'Churches Together in England' have agreed a document in the presence of the Queen at the time of her Golden Jubilee in June 2002, commiting themselves to work for unity and a 'common understanding of the message of salvation'. This was signed by Dr George Carey, Archbishop of Canterbury, Cardinal Murphy O'Connor, Roman Catholic Archbishop of Westminster, Rev. Tony Burham, Moderator of the Free Churches, and Rev. Esme Burwick, representing the smaller churches.

This raises the vital question 'Whose message of salvation will the churches reach their common understanding and unity on?' The biblical belief that salvation is a free gift granted by God granted by God to those who repent of their sins and believe in the Lord Jesus Christ, trusting in his sacrificial death on the cross for our redemption and receiving eternal life through his resurrection? Or the Roman Catholic belief in the supremacy of Church tradition over the Bible and the need for good works, penance and purgatory to attain salvation?

It is virtually certain that any union will be dictated on Rome's terms and in this we see another sign of the coming together of Christianity under the Roman Catholic umbrella with the aim of then bringing about an inter faith union of all religions. In order to counter this trend it is important that we know why the Reformation was most definitely not a mistake. The Reformers and their spiritual descendants preferred martyrdom for their faith to submitting to Roman Catholicism, believing the following to be its major errors.

Justification by works

Article 135 of the Catholic Catechism says, 'Faith alone will not save us without good works'. The Bible teaches we are saved by faith in the work of Jesus Christ dying as a sacrifice for our sins. Good works are the result of our faith, but they do not save us:

> *'For by grace you have been saved through faith, and that not of yourselves; it is the gift of God, not of works, lest anyone should boast. For we are His workmanship, created in Christ Jesus for good works, which God prepared beforehand that we should walk in them.'* (Ephesians 2:8–10)

Baptismal regeneration

Article 256 of the Catechism says, 'Baptism is a Sacrament which cleanses us from original sin, makes us Christians, children of God and members of the Church' (i.e. a baby becomes a Christian through being baptised). Article 259 says this sacrament is given by pouring water on the head of a child. (NB the Greek word *'baptizo'* means 'to immerse in water' not 'to sprinkle with water'.) It does not take long for parents of babies who have had water poured on them in this way to discover that they are not cleansed from original sin!

The Bible teaches that we must be *'born again'* (John 3:5–8) through repentance and faith in what Jesus Christ has done for us, after which we are baptised. On the Day of Pentecost Peter explained the meaning of Jesus' death and resurrection. His hearers responded by asking him, 'What shall we do?'

> *'Then Peter said to them, "Repent, and let every one of you be baptized in the name of Jesus Christ for the remission of sins; and you shall receive the gift of the Holy Spirit.'* (Acts 2:38)

A baby cannot possibly make such a decision.

Use of images

Article 186 of the Catechism says, 'We should give relics, crucifixes, and holy pictures a relative honour, as they relate to Christ and his Saints, and are memorials of them.'

Catholic churches are full of idols, especially of Mary, which become objects of worship. The Ten Commandments forbid idolatry and remain valid for Christians.

> *'You shall not make for yourself a carved image, or any likeness of anything that is in heaven above, or that is in the earth beneath, or that is in the water under the earth; you shall not bow down to them nor serve them. For I, the LORD your God, am a jealous God.'*　　　　(Exodus 20:4–5)

Papal infallibility

The Catechism says: 'When I say that the Pope is infallible, I mean that the Pope cannot err when, as Shepherd and Teacher of all Christians, he defines a doctrine concerning faith or morals, to be held by the whole church' (Article 93). The Catechism goes on to say that 'the Church cannot err in what she teaches as to faith or morals, for she is our infallible guide in both' (Article 100). The Bible tells us that only God is infallible and that all human individuals and institutions are tainted by sin and liable to error.

> *'For all have sinned and come short of the glory of God.'*
> 　　　　(Romans 3:23)

The sole authority for fixing Christian doctrine is the Bible, not fallible human beings.

The hierarchy of priests going up to the Pope as 'Vicar of Christ' on earth entirely conflicts with the concept Jesus taught the disciples about spiritual authority. Jesus told us not to call any man 'Father' (Papa/Pope).

> *'But you, do not be called "Rabbi"; for One is your Teacher, the Christ, and you are all brethren. Do not call anyone on earth your father; for One is your Father, He who is in heaven. And do not be called teachers; for One is your Teacher, the Christ. But he who is greatest among you shall be your servant.'*　　　　(Matthew 23:8–11)

Celibacy and the Priesthood

The Roman Catholic Church forbids priests to marry, thus creating a distinction between the priesthood and the laity. The word 'priest' is never used of special servants of the Lord in the New Testament, but is used to describe all who believe in Jesus. There is never any distinction in the New Testament between clergy and laity. Probably the doctrine of the Nicolaitans, mentioned in Revelation 2:6, 15, as something which Jesus hates, relates to the rise of the clergy having a special status. Nicolaitans is taken from two Greek words meaning 'victory over the people (*laos* or *laity*)'.

The New Testament teaches the priesthood of all believers.

> *'But you are a chosen generation, a royal priesthood, a holy nation, His own special people.'*   (1 Peter 2:9)

> *'And they sang a new song, saying:*
>
> *"You are worthy to take the scroll,*
> *And to open its seals;*
> *For You were slain,*
> *And have redeemed us to God by Your blood*
> *Out of every tribe and tongue and people and nation,*
> *And have made us kings and priests to our God;*
> *And we shall reign on the earth."'*
>
>   (Revelation 5:9–10)

Peter, considered falsely to be the first Pope, had a wife as the following scriptures indicate:

> *'But Simon's* [Peter's] *wife's mother lay sick with a fever, and they told Him about her at once. So He came and took her by the hand and lifted her up, and immediately the fever left her. And she served them.'*   (Mark 1:30)

> *'Do we have no right to take along a believing wife, as do also the other apostles, the brothers of the Lord, and Cephas* [Aramaic form of Peter]*?'*   (1 Corinthians 9:5)

Enforced celibacy is described as a *'doctrine of demons'*:

> *'Now the Spirit expressly says that in latter times some will depart from the faith, giving heed to deceiving spirits and doctrines of demons, speaking lies in hypocrisy, having their own conscience seared with a hot iron, forbidding to marry, and commanding to abstain from foods which God created to be received with thanksgiving by those who believe and know the truth.'*
> (1 Timothy 4:1–3)

Confession

In Catholicism people are told to go to confession, where sins are confessed to a priest who then declares absolution for those sins. The Bible teaches that we confess our sins to God and receive forgiveness through the blood of Jesus.

> *'This is the message which we have heard from Him and declare to you, that God is light and in Him is no darkness at all. If we say that we have fellowship with Him, and walk in darkness, we lie and do not practice the truth. But if we walk in the light as He is in the light, we have fellowship with one another, and the blood of Jesus Christ His Son cleanses us from all sin. If we say that we have no sin, we deceive ourselves, and the truth is not in us. If we confess our sins, He is faithful and just to forgive us our sins and to cleanse us from all unrighteousness. If we say that we have not sinned, we make Him a liar, and His word is not in us. My little children, these things I write to you, that you may not sin. And if anyone sins, we have an Advocate with the Father, Jesus Christ the righteous. And He Himself is the propitiation for our sins, and not for ours only but also for the whole world.'*
> (1 John 1:5–2:2)

Purgatory

Purgatory is neither heaven nor hell, but 'a place where souls suffer for a time after death on account of their sins'

(Catechism, Article 106). But in the Bible the only places mentioned where we go after death are heaven and hell. Those who are saved in this life by trusting in Jesus to forgive their sins need no further suffering to refine them and prepare them for heaven.

> *'And I saw a new heaven and a new earth, for the first heaven and the first earth had passed away. Also there was no more sea. Then I, John, saw the holy city, New Jerusalem, coming down out of heaven from God, prepared as a bride adorned for her husband. And I heard a loud voice from heaven saying, "Behold, the tabernacle of God is with men, and He will dwell with them, and they shall be His people, and God Himself will be with them and be their God. And God will wipe away every tear from their eyes; there shall be no more death, nor sorrow, nor crying. and there shall be no more pain, for the former things have passed away ... But the cowardly, unbelieving, abominable, murderers, sexually immoral, sorcerers, idolaters, and all liars shall have their part in the lake which burns with fire and brimstone, which is the second death."'* (Revelation 21:1–8)

Transubstantiation

According to this teaching Jesus needs to be sacrificed continually through the Mass. The bread and the wine are changed literally into his body and blood. Article 267 of the Catechism says: 'The bread and the wine are changed into the Body and Blood of Christ by the power of God, to whom nothing is impossible or difficult.' Article 278 says: 'The Holy Mass is one and the same Sacrifice with that of the Cross, inasmuch as Christ who offered himself, a bleeding victim on the Cross to his heavenly Father, continues to offer himself in an unbloody manner on the altar through the ministry of his priests.'

But the Bible teaches that Christ's sacrifice was complete and final and can never be repeated. Communion or the Lord's Supper is the remembrance of that sacrifice.

'For Christ has not entered the holy places made with hands, which are copies of the true, but into heaven itself, now to appear in the presence of God for us; not that He should offer Himself often, as the high priest enters the Most Holy Place every year with blood of another – He then would have had to suffer often since the foundation of the world; but now, once at the end of the ages, He has appeared to put away sin by the sacrifice of Himself. And as it is appointed for men to die once, but after this the judgment, so Christ was offered once to bear the sins of many.'   (Hebrews 9:24–28)

'For I received from the Lord that which I also delivered to you: that the Lord Jesus on the same night in which He was betrayed took bread; and when He had given thanks, He broke it and said, "Take, eat; this is My body which is broken for you; do this in remembrance of Me." In the same manner He also took the cup after supper, saying, "This cup is the new covenant in My blood. This do, as often as you drink it, in remembrance of Me." For as often as you eat this bread and drink this cup, you proclaim the Lord's death till He comes.'   (1 Corinthians 11:23–26)

Indulgences

In the Middle Ages priests went throughout Europe persuading people to give money to the Church claiming that as a result a person's time in purgatory could be reduced. But since there is no such place as purgatory, this became a trick to deceive people into parting with their money for the benefit of the Church. There is no way that we can buy favour with God.

'Knowing that you were not redeemed with corruptible things, like silver or gold, from your aimless conduct received by tradition from your fathers, but with the precious blood of Christ, as of a lamb without blemish and without spot.'
                    (1 Peter 1:18–19)

Penance

It was also taught that by inflicting pain and torment on one's body one could reduce time in purgatory. Self-inflicted suffering to atone for our sins is of no value at all, since Christ's sufferings are enough to redeem us.

> *'For Christ also suffered once for sins, the just for the unjust, that He might bring us to God, being put to death in the flesh but made alive by the Spirit.'* (1 Peter 3:18)

Self-denial from sins of the flesh is of course taught in the Bible.

Mariolatry

The Roman Catholic Church elevates Mary to the status of 'mother of God' (Catechism, Article 167) and 'Queen of Heaven' (Article 168a). As a result Mary becomes a 'co-Redemptrix' worshipped alongside or above Jesus, as can be seen by the size of the images of the Madonna in many Catholic Churches. Article 117 says: 'All mankind has contracted the guilt and stain of original sin, except The Blessed Virgin and her Divine Son.'

Mary was in fact a faithful Jewish woman called Miriam who played a vital role in bringing Jesus into the world through the miracle of the virgin birth. There is not a word in the New Testament suggesting she was sinless or had a different nature from other people. After giving birth to Jesus, she had other children in the natural way and was saved by her faith in her Son, the Lord Jesus. There are a number of references in the New Testament to Jesus' brothers and sisters.

> *'These all continued with one accord in prayer and supplication, with the women and Mary the mother of Jesus, and with His brothers.'* (Acts 1:14)

There is no other mediator between God and man except the Lord Jesus.

> *'For there is one God and one Mediator between God and men, the Man Christ Jesus, who gave Himself a ransom for all.'*   (1 Timothy 2:5–6)

Further information

Tony Pearce produces a quarterly magazine, *Light for the Last Days* which gives up to date information on the kind of issues covered in this book. He also produces a monthly tape, *This Month in Prophecy* which deals with major events of prophetic significance that have happened in the previous month.

He leads 'The Bridge Christian Fellowship' in North West London.

For follow-up Bible study send for *The Omega Course* (also available in French). 60p plus postage.

To receive any of the information please contact:

Tony Pearce
Light for the Last Days
Box BM-4226
London WC1N 3XX

e-mail: enquiries@lightforthelastdays.co.uk
Website: http://www.lightforthelastdays.co.uk